Mary Berry is known to m
networked Thames Television
regular contributor to BBC *Wo*
in BBC and local radio phone-i

Mary Berry was, for several _____, _____ _____ __ *Ideal Home* and is now a regular contributor to *Family Circle*. She is one of Britain's most popular cookery writers and has written over twenty books.

By the same author

MARY BERRY'S

New Cake Book

Grafton Books

A Division of HarperCollins*Publishers*

GraftonBooks
A Division of HarperCollins*Publishers*
77–85 Fulham Palace Road,
Hammersmith, London W6 8JB

Published by GraftonBooks 1991
9 8 7 6 5 4 3 2 1

First published in Great Britain by
Judy Piatkus (Publishers) Limited 1989

A CIP catalogue record for this book
is available from the British Library

ISBN 0-586-21044-X

Printed in Great Britain by
HarperCollinsManufacturing Glasgow

Set in Century Schoolbook

DEDICATION

For months now our cake tins and freezer have been at bursting point with goodies. The young have certainly revelled in the bounty of this book. My special thanks to Debbie Woolhead, Sheila Inglis and Joanna Drew who have helped with the testing, typing and – most important of all – the tasting.

CONTENTS

INTRODUCTION

Each year more and more new cake-making books are published, and my own *Fast Cakes* and *More Fast Cakes* have both proved a great success.

Therefore it seemed a good idea to put together a new collection of my favourite recipes. Some will be familiar, but they have been adapted to cater for the new awareness of healthier eating. Most are new and, between them they cover every baking occasion.

I have included cakes for everyday for the family cake tin, to be raided when the children come home from school, and for tea after those brisk walks at the weekend. Traybakes, although good for everyday as well, are most practical to make and sell in pieces at bring-and-buy sales, local fêtes or school bazaars. (It's very satisfying making these, I think, as everyone always makes a beeline for you and your wares!) There are cakes for desserts, creamy and chocolaty, to serve as a magnificent finale to a lunch or dinner party. Many cakes are traditional at times of special celebration – at Easter, Christmas, or for birthdays, weddings, christenings and anniversaries – and there is a wide selection here. Children love to help with cake making, and I've included a few recipes for junior cake fans.

Many people think, mistakenly, that cake making is difficult. It certainly is a more precise method of cooking than any other, but if you follow the recipes accurately, keeping several general 'rules' in mind, you should be able to enjoy success every time. And if you have an enthusiastic response to one recipe, don't hesitate to make it again – you could become famed for it!

I hope you enjoy the selection here, and I wish you happy baking.

Mary Berry

November 1988

BETTER CAKE MAKING

Baking Tins

I list below the tins I have used in the recipes throughout the book, but if you want to adapt a recipe to a different container, use this simple method of measuring. To bake an 8 inch (20 cm) cake in a ring-mould tin, for instance, fill the standard cake tin with water up to where the top of the cake mixture would be, then pour into the ring mould. If the water comes over the top, so will the mixture. (Cooking time in a ring-mould tin will be less because the sides conduct the heat better through the cake.)

The cake tins I like best are Pullman pans, made by Pullman Pans Ltd, Eastfield Industrial Estate, Penicuik, EH26 8HA. They are aluminium, anodized black, silicone glazed and are non-stick, so don't need to be lined. They conduct heat very well as the black lining absorbs the heat. I've had mine for nine years now, and wouldn't be without them. If you're a keen baker, they'll be well worth the initial investment.

Lacking Pullman pans, I would prefer to use loose-bottomed cake tins, because they are easier to turn out and there is no need to line them. But if yours aren't loose-bottomed, don't panic; I tell you on page 13 how and when to line tins.

All the recipes use one or other of the following tins.

2 × 7 inch (18 cm) round sandwich tins (best with loose bases)
1 × 7 inch (18 cm) deep round cake tin (best with loose base)
2 × 7 inch (18 cm) square cake tins
1 × 7 inch (18 cm) shallow square tin
2 × 8 inch (20 cm) round sandwich tins (best with loose bases)
1 × 8 inch (20 cm) deep round cake tin (best with loose base)
1 × 8 inch (20 cm) square cake tin
1 × 8 inch (20 cm) shallow square tin

1 × 8 inch (20 cm) sponge flan tin or dish
1 × 9 inch (23 cm) deep round cake tin (best with loose base)
1 × 9 inch (23 cm) loose-bottomed flan tin
1 × 9 inch (23 cm) heart-shaped tin
2 × 1 lb (450 g) loaf tins
1 × 2 lb (900 g) loaf tin
1 × 11 × 7 inch (28 × 18 cm) Swiss roll tin
1 × 12 × 8 inch (30 × 20 cm) Swiss roll tin
1 × 13 × 9 inch (33 × 23 cm) Swiss roll tin
1 × 12 × 9 inch (30 × 23 cm) roasting tin
2–3 patty or bun tins
2 large, heavy, flat metal baking trays
tartlet moulds (if you have them, or you can use the patty tins)
baba ring moulds (an extravagance, but worth it for a special
    treat!)

If you haven't any cake tins – but I hope that after reading
some of the recipes in the book you'll want to invest in some –
you can improvise. Look for something like an ovenglass soufflé
dish with straight sides and cover it on the outside with a
double layer of foil, folding and pressing it in to fit snugly. Take
the foil 'baking tin' off the dish and stand on a baking tray.
Grease it and fill with your mixture. Similarly, if you have only
one baking tin, and the recipe requires two, you can make its
twin as above.

Another necessity is a cooling rack, or two, on which to turn out
the baked cakes to cool. The grid from your grill pan could be
used.

A final tip on baking tins. If you take cakes in tins or trays to a
jumble or bring-and-buy sale etc., write your name on the
bottom of them with a waterproof marker. That way you'll
always get your own tins back.

Preparation Equipment

Cake making doesn't require much equipment that won't
already be in your kitchen.

SCALES

A good pair of weighing scales is vital for making cakes. Although your grandmother may never have weighed her ingredients and simply tossed in a handful of this and a handful of that, she was doing it by instinct. And unless you possess the same instinct, you *must* weigh accurately. Baking, more than any other branch of cookery, involves chemistry – exact proportions of ingredients reacting with each other – and it would be a shame to spoil a mixture for want of a little initial patience.

I use electronic battery scales which, when you put a bowl on, strike back to the nought again. They are free standing, and all you have to do is replace the batteries occasionally.

MEASURES

A selection of accurate measuring spoons are vital, and all the amounts given in the recipes are for level spoonfuls. Use a see-through measuring jug for liquids.

BOWLS

A selection of different sized mixing bowls, preferably oven-glass, are necessary for mixing the ingredients.

FOOD MIXER

Both hand and electric versions are useful. Follow the instructions in the handbook.

FOOD PROCESSOR

These are increasingly used and are very timesaving. In making cakes, however, you can easily *over*mix, and things like nuts or dried fruit can be processed to nothing!

WOODEN SPOONS

One at least is useful, but it should have a rounded bowl to get into the curves of mixing bowls.

WOODEN SPATULA

I prefer using a spatula to a spoon to mix cake mixtures. It is flat on both sides and extremely easy to scrape clean!

FISH SLICE
This is useful for lifting out traybakes and also lifting biscuits off baking trays.

WHISK
A small or medium wire balloon whisk can be used for light mixtures, or for egg yolks, whites or small amounts of cream – rather easier and quicker in many cases than using an electrical gadget.

SCRAPER
A plastic or rubber scraper is useful for getting all of a mixture off the sides of the bowl into the tin. This is not popular with the children, though, as there isn't much of the mixture left for them to lick!

KNIVES
A palette knife is useful for spreading icing over cakes. A long, very sharp knife, preferably serrated, is vital for cutting a cake cleanly into layers – an operation used in many of the recipes following.

ALUMINIUM FOIL
Aluminium foil can be used to line baking trays and/or tins, the latter for when more strength is needed (or indeed when you *haven't* any tins, see above). It's also useful in traybakes; leave 'tails' at either end, and you can easily lift the whole thing out. Use the narrower rolls of foil in baking; the 'turkey' sizes will be too big and you'll be wasteful.

Foil can be used too, as on page 137, to make a 'cake board'.

GREASEPROOF PAPER
This is what I use normally for lining cake tins which don't have loose bottoms. It should be of good quality, and is available in sheets and rolls.

SILICONE PAPER
This is sometimes called Bakewell paper (the manufacturer's

name) or vegetable non-stick parchment. It is available in packets of sheets or on the roll. For me, it is a must for things containing a high proportion of sugar, such as meringues. If you line the baking tray with silicone paper, the meringues will never stick and the paper can be used again and again – simply shake off the sugar and put it back in the packet.

PULLMAN PAPER
This is made by the same people that make the baking pans. It is used by commercial bakers, and should soon be generally available. It is a black, stiff, polythene-type material which comes in sheets, is non-stick, and can be used again and again.

CLEAR FILM
This cannot be used in baking, of course, but it is useful for lining the tins or trays of some types of non-bake cakes. A chilled or frozen cake comes out of its tin easily if you leave flaps of clear film at the top which you can get hold of.

PAPER CASES
There are various types, larger for small buns and very small for petits fours (or the truffles on page 77). I don't place them willy-nilly on a baking tray, as they become misshapen when the mix is poured or spooned in. Place them inside bun or patty tins and then fill them.

Storage Equipment

A freezer is perhaps the ultimate store for cakes if they're not to be eaten straight away. Here they keep in perfect condition, safe from thieving fingers. A cake made some weeks before, frozen then defrosted, can be the trouble-free and time-saving centrepiece of a tea or dinner party. See page 16 for information on freezing cakes.

CLEAR FILM
This is useful for storing cakes. Wrapping a cake in film both keeps the moisture in and enables you to identify what it is!

ALUMINIUM FOIL

This too is useful for storing cakes if you do not have airtight tins. Simply wrap them completely in foil to protect them and keep in the moisture. It can also be used for placing between layers of cakes in storage tins.

AIRTIGHT STORAGE TINS

Vital for biscuits, so that they don't go soft. Never store cakes and biscuits together – the latter will absorb some moisture from the former and go soft.

You can buy tins especially for storing cakes and biscuits, but often bought biscuits or other goodies come in tins which can be adapted for cake or biscuit storage. If a lid isn't quite airtight enough, use a piece of foil to make the fit perfect.

POLYTHENE BAGS

Polythene bags can be used for cake storage too, and the special freezer ones are stronger if you're freezing your cakes, or any cake ingredients. Greased bags are also placed over and around yeasted cakes and pastries during rising.

Cake Ingredients

If you want to make cakes that taste as fresh and good as possible, use the best quality ingredients. It's as simple as that.

BUTTERS AND MARGARINES

I love butter, but I only use it in cakes where the flavour will come through. Shortbread is an example, but I must admit I often use half butter and half margarine. Forget about unsalted butter – it's too expensive!

I use both block (hard) margarines and soft, but do not use low-fat soft margarines when heat is involved, as they disintegrate because of their high water content. Be careful to buy those margarines which are suitable for baking. Low-fat margarines can be used for butter creams.

Soft margarines simplify the baking process as you don't have to allow time for softening.

FLOURS
I usually use McDougalls self-raising and plain flours for cakes, and strong plain flours for richer pastries and bread. Allinson's wholemeal and wheatmeal, plain and self-raising, are excellent.

For shortbread, I always like to use a proportion of cornflour, semolina or rice flour which gives a gritty crunch and adds to the texture. (For a yellow shortbread made with cornflour, you can add a ½ teaspoon of custard powder!)

RAISING AGENTS
I use Borwick's baking powder as I find other varieties sometimes come in different strengths. Too much baking powder can spoil the texture and flavour of a cake, so use only the amount stated in the recipe.

Yeast is available fresh and dried, but I now use the easy-blend dried yeast in bread, cakes or pastries.

SUGARS
I like to use the more natural sugars such as golden caster and golden granulated. I also like muscovado sugar, particularly the light – the dark has too strong a flavour. I still use demerara, as it is good to sprinkle on the tops of cakes, and of course icing sugar must be used for icing.

Vanilla sugar   Several of my recipes call for this. It is simply caster sugar stored in a jar with two or three vanilla pods. After a couple of weeks, the sugar is imbued with the flavour of the vanilla; as you use the sugar, simply top up the jar with more.

EGGS
All the eggs used in this book are size 3 unless otherwise noted. Eggs keep best in the refrigerator or cold larder, but be sure to bring them to room temperature before using.

If you keep ducks, you can use their eggs in recipes, depending on size.

CREAM

I never use synthetic creams. Double cream doesn't feature much in my recipes either because, being full fat, it is too thick for most purposes. For cakes, use whipping cream which is cheaper – and for reasons of both health and economy, I often use half whipped cream and half low-fat plain yoghurt. Cream is best whipped from cold.

YOGHURT

You can use low- or full-fat natural or plain yoghurt, whichever you please. The full-fat variety or Greek-style yoghurt has the best flavour.

CREAM CHEESE

For cheesecakes, use low-fat or full-fat soft cheese, whichever you like. I often add some cream to low-fat cheese to make it richer. I never use cottage cheese put through the processor or blender.

CHOCOLATE

For the best and most concentrated chocolate flavour, use cocoa powder. This is produced from cocoa butter – the fats of the cacao bean. Drinking chocolate, which is diluted in flavour and sweetened, should never be used as a substitute. You can use an eating chocolate such as Bournville, which performs well in cooking and has a good flavour. I never use chocolate 'drops', and I only use a cooking chocolate, the chocolate cake covering, when I want to make curls. Cooking chocolate does not contain cocoa butter, so the flavour isn't good, but it melts and curls easily.

Chocolate curls　Also known as caraque. Melt chocolate cake covering in a bowl over a pan of hot water, then spread very thinly on to a clean, scratchproof work surface and leave until nearly set. Then, with a long sharp knife, shave it off the surface, using a slight sawing action and holding the knife almost upright so that the chocolate forms scrolls or flakes.

ESSENCES AND FLAVOURINGS

I can't see why one should use an essence when the real thing is so often to hand – fresh lemons or rum, for instance. I would always use vanilla sugar if appropriate (see above), rather than essence. Camp coffee is good for a coffee flavour, and if using instant coffee, powder or granules, this needs to be dissolved first in a little hot water.

NUTS

Ground, flaked or split nuts for use in baking are expensive, and do not keep for very long in a warm modern kitchen. My solution is to freeze them, well wrapped, for up to a year. When you want to use some, take out what you need, returning the remainder to the freezer. Whole shelled nuts can also be frozen, for up to five years.

Before using whole almonds or hazelnuts in baking, the skins need to be removed. Roast hazelnuts briefly in the oven, and then rub off the skins; immerse almonds in boiling water until the skins slip off. Chop them either by hand with a sharp knife, or in the processor – but watch that you don't *over*-process.

DRIED FRUIT

These too can dry out in a warm kitchen, so I store them in a big polythene bag in the freezer. Mixed peel keeps better this way, and dried apricots don't darken in colour.

If you do a lot of baking, you can buy the fruits separately – raisins, currants, peel, etc – and mix up your own mixed fruit in the proportions you like.

Glacé cherries should always be washed and thoroughly dried before putting in a cake mixture, as this prevents them sinking to the bottom.

CITRUS RIND

When grating rind for a cake – whether of orange or lemon – first wash and dry the fruit well. Grate the rind on the small-holed side of the grater, making sure you scrape it all off the grater, and add immediately to the sugar content of the recipe. The rind doesn't discolour by doing this, and the oils of the rind will be absorbed by the sugar.

GELATINE

I use the powdered variety. Add the water to the powder in a small bowl or handleless cup, stir it and it will set like a sponge in a few minutes. Heat it through gently by putting the bowl or cup in a pan of very gently simmering water. When it becomes clear it is ready to use.

Cake Making

Most of the cake-making instructions are attached to individual cake recipes, but there are a few general hints which are gathered together here.

PREPARING A CAKE MIXTURE

First make sure that you have all the listed ingredients, the necessary tins, and the *time* to make and bake the cake. If you have to nip out to collect the children from school or do some shopping, prepare and weigh out the ingredients, then *come back* to your 'operating table'. This way is much better than hurrying and perhaps spoiling the cake.

Weigh out the ingredients carefully, following the order given in the recipe listing, ticking them off if you like so that no ingredient is accidentally forgotten.

Mix the ingredients by hand or in the processor or mixer, whichever you prefer, following the recipe or machine instructions, or your own instincts or expertise. Continue mixing until the mixture is the specified colour or texture – the success of the finished cake depends on this.

My all-in-one cakes are exactly that. Everything goes into the container – bowl, pan or mixer – at the same time. Do use self-raising flour *and* baking powder for these cakes. The speed of the method means that there is not so much air beaten into the mixture as with traditional cakes, and the baking powder gives that necessary lift. (However, using *more* baking powder than specified will not help – it will make it worse in fact.)

You can adapt your own recipes to the all-in-one method. Add 1 level teaspoon baking powder to every 4 oz (100 g) self-raising flour.

LINING CAKE TINS

If a cake tin has a loose base, all you need to do is grease the base and sides. For tins without a loose base, you'll need to grease *and* line the bottom of the tin with greaseproof paper. If a cake mix is rich – a rich fruit cake for example – you'll need to grease and line both base and sides.

Bases For both round and square tins – and indeed any other shaped tin – put the base of the tin on a piece of greaseproof paper and draw in pencil around it. Cut out, just inside the pencilled line. Grease the base and sides of the tin, then insert the disc, square or whatever into the tin. Grease all surfaces again.

Sides Cut strips of greaseproof paper which are 1–1½ inches (2.5–4 cm) wider than the depth or height of the tin. The strips should be long enough to go completely around the sides of the tin, whether round, square or heart-shaped. Fold over a good ½ inch (1.25 cm) along one whole length of the strip. Open out the fold and cut slanting lines through the narrow fold bit, precisely to the fold line. Fit this strip into the tin, with the slashed strip folding over on to the bottom of the tin. Then fit in the base disc or square *over* the slashes, and the tin is fully lined.

Another way of lining a square or rectangular tin, deep or shallow, is to stand the tin on a large piece of greaseproof paper, at least the size of the tin and its depth. Mark with pencil around the base and then measure and rule in lines outside this which correspond to the *depth* of the tin. Cut at an angle from outer corner to inner corner at all four corners then fit the paper in the greased tin. The cut corners will overlap, and excess can be cut away. Grease again.

A time-saving tip for those among you who bake often: cut several base discs or squares at the same time and keep them in the kitchen drawer in a polythene bag, ready for use at a moment's notice.

BAKING CAKES
The first necessity is to preheat the oven to the correct temperature. If you use gas or electricity, you must allow time for this. The correct oven temperature is vital for cake-making success, and if you're uncertain of your oven, buy or borrow an oven thermometer, and check it yourself.

Before turning on the oven, you may first have to adjust the position of the oven shelves, depending on the type of oven you have. If baking one cake, use the shelf in the centre position; if baking two cakes, one cake is usually on a shelf above centre, the other below. Check your cooker instructions for baking cakes though: in theory, a good oven should cook equally throughout; in practice ovens do differ.

• Never open the oven door or move the cake tin during the first stages of baking, as both these actions will make the cake sink in the middle.

• If you're baking several things at the same time, they will take longer to cook than a solitary cake. Keep an eye on them in the later stages.

• If anything ever looks as though it might be browning too much too early, place a sheet of foil loosely over the top.

TELLING WHEN A CAKE IS DONE
The principal signs of done-ness for most cakes are when the cake shrinks slightly from the sides of the tin and when the top of the cake springs back after being pressed lightly with the finger. The look and the smell can also be informative.

Fruit cakes need another test, which is to push a skewer into the centre. If the skewer comes out clean, the cake is ready; if there is some cake mixture adhering to the skewer, it needs a little longer – but check carefully. If a cake such as this looks as though it's browning too much on the top, cover with foil and cook for a bit longer at a lower temperature.

Meringues should be crisp or the colour specified in the recipe. Check biscuits and shortbreads by eye, and look underneath as well.

COOLING CAKES

Particular cooling instructions are attached to individual recipes. In general, though, leave cakes in the tin to contract, firm up and cool for a while before turning them out on to a wire rack to become completely cold. This prevents them sticking or perhaps breaking.

• Before turning out, run a knife quickly round the edges of the cake tin.

• To turn a cake out of a loose-bottomed tin, stand the base on something like a large can so that the side can slip down, leaving the cake free, still standing on the tin base.

• If the tin has been lined, peel off the paper very carefully. Special care is needed for thinner cakes such as roulades or Swiss rolls.

• Victoria sponges I turn out on to a rack and then replace the tins over them. This prevents the moisture evaporating while the cakes are cooling, but doesn't make them soggy.

• Leave meringues in the turned-off oven to cool. This dries them out further. Then simply slip off the silicone paper.

• Don't leave biscuits to cool on a tray until stone cold, or they'll stick. Remove with a palette knife or fish slice while still warm, peeling off the paper.

• Certain cakes such as shortbreads and flapjacks are not cooled on a cooling tray as this spoils their texture.

KEEPING CAKES

In general, few cakes improve with keeping, except perhaps for gingerbread and, of course, celebration or richer fruit cakes. More frugal fruit cakes are best eaten when freshly made, as are sponge cakes and flan cases.

The place to keep cakes for their short life is in an airtight storage tin. Meringues will store in a tin for at least a week.

However, many cakes can be frozen, well wrapped, either whole or in pieces: a couple of slices wrapped separately could defrost happily for a lunchbox or an unexpected visitor at tea or coffee time. Mince pies too can be frozen, and there's no need to thaw them – just heat through in the oven and serve hot. Freeze cakes for no longer than three months, as I've found that after this they tend to lose a little of their flavour when thawed out.

For freezing, wrap cakes in foil or in polythene bags. Larger, more delicate cakes can be polythene-wrapped in boxes to avoid crushing.

ICING AND DECORATING CAKES

Icings, fillings and decorations can transform the simplest of cakes. First of all, though, the cake must be absolutely cold.

A simple glacé icing is made from well-sifted icing sugar and a liquid, often lemon juice, occasionally water. Go easy with the liquid as it is very easy to add too much; if the icing is runny just sift in more sugar. The quantity is individually specified in most recipes.

When colouring a glacé icing, do so with extreme care, as colour darkens when the icing sets. Dip a cocktail stick in red food colouring, for instance, and drip in drop by drop to give an icing that's the required pale pink colour rather than pillarbox red!

Other icings are fondant and royal, and I give recipes for these on pages 124–5.

● Keep any icing covered with a piece of damp cloth or clear film so that the surface does not dry out and form lumps.

● If you can be bothered, brush a cake to be iced with some apricot glaze first. This is simply whole or strained apricot jam, and it's gently heated to make it runny. The use of this glaze – which 'sets' when cold – means that cake crumbs won't find their way into the icing as it is being spread; neither will the icing become dull, because the cake won't so readily absorb the moisture in the icing. Apricot glaze is also useful for making things stick – almond paste to a celebration cake, for instance.

● If you want to pipe icing or whipped cream on to a cake, you can use a proper nozzle and piping bag (rinse the latter, and wash in the machine with your whites), or improvise with a polythene bag snipped at the corner. To fill a proper piping bag, stand it in a jug point down, and bend the top edges over the top of the jug, leaving a large opening into which the mixture can easily be spooned.

Top Favourite Family Cakes

There is an interesting selection of cake recipes here, some familiar, some less usual, some simple, some slightly more complicated. All of them are delicious, both for everyday eating – when hunger strikes, when the children return from school – and for more special occasions. They are the sort of cakes you could make on a Friday for the weekend, ideal for Saturday or Sunday tea in front of the fire after a long bracing walk. In fact, they are good-to-come-home-to cakes!

My family used to ensure enthusiastically that there was nothing left of a cake at the end of the weekend. Even now, although the boys are away from home, their weekend visits invariably result in remnants of cake being wrapped up to take back with them. But if you are left with some sponge cake, freeze it in wedges, or serve with cream for a pudding on Monday. Fruit cake leftovers freeze well too.

MADEIRA CAKE

This cake is the one which traditionally accompanies Verdelho, one of the sweet wines from Madeira. I always used to make Madeira cake with butter, but I find the new soft margarines give a really well-flavoured result.

8 oz (225 g) self-raising flour   finely grated rind of 1 lemon
6 oz (175 g) soft margarine   a strip of lemon citron peel,
7 oz (200 g) caster sugar   washed and dried (optional)
4 eggs

Heat the oven to 350°F, 180°C, gas mark 4. Grease and line a 7 inch (18 cm) round cake tin with greased greaseproof paper.

Measure all the ingredients, except for the peel, into a bowl and beat well until smooth. Spread the mixture in the prepared tin and level.

Bake for 30 minutes until set, then carefully lift the peel on to the cake. Reduce the oven temperature to 325°F, 160°C, gas mark 3, and cook for a further hour. (Total cooking time, 1½ hours.) The cake should be shrinking away slightly from the sides of the tin and be pale golden in colour.

Cool in the tin for about 10 minutes, then turn out, peel off paper, and finish cooling on a wire rack.

BUTTER ALMOND CAKE

A lovely light cake, perfect to serve for Sunday tea.

6 oz (175 g) butter, softened
6 oz (175 g) caster sugar
4 eggs, beaten
4 oz (100 g) ground almonds
7 oz (200 g) self-raising flour

1 teaspoon almond essence

Topping
1 oz (25 g) flaked almonds

Heat the oven to 350°F, 180°C, gas mark 4. Grease and line an 8 inch (20 cm) deep round cake tin with greased greaseproof paper.

Measure the butter and sugar into a bowl and beat well until light and fluffy. Beat in the eggs a little at a time. Gently fold in the almonds, flour and almond essence until thoroughly blended. Turn into the prepared tin and level out evenly. Scatter flaked almonds over the top.

Bake in the oven for about 1¼ hours until well risen and golden brown. A skewer should come out clean when pushed into the centre of the cake.

Leave to cool in the tin for a few minutes, then turn out, peel off paper and finish cooling on a wire rack.

VICTORIA SANDWICH CAKE

One of the classic cakes to serve for tea, and it can be flavoured in different ways – see the variations that follow. This amount of mixture makes a good deep sandwich. It is remarkably quick to make, just beating the ingredients together in one bowl. If you are making the sandwich to freeze, I prefer to freeze unfilled, slipping a piece of silicone or greaseproof paper between the sandwiches and then wrapping in foil. To thaw, loosen the wrapping and leave at room temperature for 3 hours. Then fill and leave to thaw completely before serving.

If cooking several cakes in the oven at one time, for school fêtes or bazaars, allow a little longer baking time. You may also have to turn them in the oven to get perfect even baking; do not do this until 5 minutes before the end of the cooking time, otherwise the cakes will sink as the mixture will not be set.

6 oz (175 g) soft margarine
6 oz (175 g) caster sugar
3 eggs, beaten
6 oz (175 g) self-raising flour

1½ teaspoons baking powder

Filling and Topping
about 4 tablespoons
   strawberry or raspberry
   jam
a little caster sugar

Heat the oven to 350°F, 180°C, gas mark 4. Grease and line two 7 inch (18 cm) round sandwich tins with greased greaseproof paper.

Measure the margarine, sugar, eggs, flour and baking powder into a large bowl and beat well until thoroughly blended. Divide the mixture between the two tins and level out evenly.

Bake in the oven for about 25 minutes until well risen, and the tops of the cakes spring back when lightly pressed with a finger. Leave to cool in the tins for a few moments then turn out, peel off paper and finish cooling on a wire rack.

When completely cold, sandwich the two cakes together with the jam. Lift on to a serving plate and serve sprinkled with a little caster sugar.

ORANGE OR LEMON

Add the finely grated rind of 1 orange or 1 lemon to the cake mixture. Serve sandwiched together with lemon curd or orange marmalade.

CHOCOLATE

Blend 2 tablespoons sieved cocoa with 3 tablespoons boiling water in the mixing bowl. Cool, then add the remaining ingredients and continue as above. (There is no need to decrease the amount of flour in the recipe.) Sandwich together with white butter cream: blend together 2 oz (50 g) soft margarine, 6 oz (175 g) sieved icing sugar and 1 tablespoon milk.

COFFEE

Dissolve 2 heaped teaspoons instant coffee in the beaten eggs before adding to the bowl. Sandwich the cakes together with coffee butter cream: add 1 tablespoon coffee essence to the white butter cream in the chocolate cake recipe above.

COFFEE FUDGE CAKE

A rich and delicious cake, with an easy-to-make fudge icing. Serve it in slim wedges.

6 oz (175 g) soft margarine
6 oz (175 g) caster sugar
3 eggs
1 tablespoon coffee essence
6 oz (175 g) self-raising flour
1½ level teaspoons baking
   powder

8 oz (225 g) icing sugar, sieved
1 tablespoon milk
1 tablespoon coffee essence

Decoration
a few chocolate coffee beans or
   shelled walnuts

Filling and Icing
3 oz (75 g) soft margarine

Heat the oven to 350°F, 180°C, gas mark 4. Grease and line two 8 inch (20 cm) sandwich tins with greased greaseproof paper.

Measure all the ingredients for the cake into a bowl and beat well until thoroughly blended. Divide the mixture between the two tins and level out evenly.

Bake in the oven for about 30 minutes until well risen and shrinking away slightly from the sides of the tins. Allow to cool for a few minutes, then turn out, peel off paper and finish cooling on a wire rack.

For the filling and icing, measure all the ingredients into a bowl and beat well until thoroughly blended. Use half the mixture to sandwich the two cakes together, then stand on a serving plate and spread the remaining mixture on top. Mark decoratively with a fork and arrange some chocolate coffee beans or shelled walnuts on top.

WHOLEWHEAT LEMON CAKE

For a less rich cake, simply sandwich the cakes together with 3 tablespoons lemon curd blended with 3 tablespoons natural yoghurt. If you like a deeper cake, bake in two 7 inch (18 cm) sandwich tins.

6 oz (175 g) soft margarine	grated rind of 1 lemon
6 oz (175 g) light muscovado sugar	2 tablespoons milk
3 eggs	*Filling and Topping*
6 oz (175 g) self-raising wholewheat flour	3 oz (75 g) soft margarine
	8 oz (225 g) icing sugar, sieved
1½ level teaspoons baking powder	3 tablespoons lemon juice

Heat the oven to 350°F, 180°C, gas mark 4, and grease and line two 8 inch (20 cm) sandwich tins with greased greaseproof paper.

Measure all the ingredients for the cake into a bowl and beat well for about 2 minutes, until smooth and blended. Divide the mixture between the two tins and level out evenly.

Bake in the oven for about 25–30 minutes. When cooked, the cakes will have shrunk away slightly from the sides of the tin, and will spring back when lightly pressed with a finger. Turn the sponges out on to a wire rack to cool. Peel off the paper.

For the filling and topping, measure all the ingredients into a bowl and blend together until smooth. Use half to sandwich the cakes together and spread the remainder on top. Mark decoratively with a fork and allow to set.

SIMPLE ORANGE CAKE

Use a fine grater to grate the orange rind. Wrap the leftover oranges in clear film and keep in the fridge for a couple of days; use as freshly squeezed orange juice, or for a sauce. For a deeper cake, use two 7 inch (18 cm) sandwich tins.

6 oz (175 g) soft margarine
6 oz (175 g) caster sugar
3 eggs
6 oz (175 g) self-raising flour
grated rind of 2 small oranges
2 level teaspoons baking
 powder

icing sugar, to dust

Butter Cream
3 oz (75 g) butter
4 oz (100 g) icing sugar, sieved
grated rind of 1 orange

Grease and line two 8 inch (20 cm) sandwich tins with greased greaseproof paper, and heat the oven to 350°F, 180°C, gas mark 4.

For the cake, measure all the ingredients, except for the icing sugar, into a bowl and beat well for about 2 minutes, until thoroughly blended. Divide the mixture between the two tins and level out evenly.

Bake in the oven for about 35 minutes until shrinking away from the sides of the tin slightly, and the sponges are golden brown.

Leave to cool in the tins for a few moments then turn out, peel off paper and finish cooling on a wire rack.

For the butter cream, measure the ingredients into a bowl and cream together until blended, adding a little orange juice to soften the mixture if necessary. Use to sandwich the two cakes together. Serve dusted with a little icing sugar.

GRANARY SQUARES

As well as the crunchy sugar topping expect to find crunchy bits from the granary flour in the squares too. These are delicious with morning coffee – or indeed with afternoon tea!

4 oz (100 g) soft margarine
4 oz (100 g) light muscovado
   sugar
4 oz (100 g) granary flour
2 oz (50 g) self-raising flour

2 teaspoons baking powder
2 tablespoons milk
6 oz (175 g) mixed dried fruit
2 good tablespoons demerara
   sugar

Heat the oven to 375°F, 190°C, gas mark 5 and line a shallow 8 inch (20 cm) square tin (or a small roasting tin) with greased greaseproof paper or foil. Grease it well.

Measure all the ingredients *except* for the demerara sugar into a bowl and mix until smooth. Spread out into the tin and bake for about 30 minutes until it shrinks away from the sides and is pale golden in colour. Sprinkle with demerara sugar and return to the oven just long enough to melt the sugar, probably about 5 minutes. Leave in the tin to cool. Cut into squares.

Makes 16 pieces

BATTENBURG CAKES

This recipe makes two cakes. I now use bought almond paste as I find it is just as good as making your own. Choose a good quality one, but if you're still determined to make your own see page 122.

8 oz (225 g) soft margarine
8 oz (225 g) caster sugar
4 eggs
4 oz (100 g) semolina
8 oz (225 g) self-raising flour
1½ level teaspoons baking powder

¼ teaspoon almond essence
2 tablespoons milk
red food colouring
apricot jam
1 lb (450 g) almond paste (or see page 122)

Heat the oven to 325°F, 160°C, gas mark 3. Grease and line two 7 inch (18 cm) square cake tins with greased greaseproof paper.

Measure the margarine, sugar, eggs, semolina, flour, baking powder, almond essence and milk into a bowl and beat well until thoroughly blended. Spread *half* of this mixture into one of the tins.

Add a few drops of food colouring to the remaining mixture and mix well until evenly blended and a deep pink colour. Spread this into the second tin and level the top.

Bake both cakes in the oven for about 40 minutes until well risen and shrinking back slightly from the sides of the tins. Allow to cool for a few moments then turn out, peel off paper and finish cooling on a wire rack.

To assemble the cakes, trim the edges of each cake and cut each into four strips. Using the apricot jam, stick together a pink and white strip lengthways, then stick two other strips on top, lengthways, to create a chequered pattern. Make two cakes in this way.

Divide the almond paste in two and roll out each piece to an oblong the length of the cakes and sufficiently wide to wrap right the way round the cakes. Brush the tops of the cakes with apricot jam and place them inverted on the almond paste. Brush the remaining sides with jam and wrap the almond paste round and make a neat seal. Invert the right way up, seal beneath. Mark a criss-cross pattern on the top of the cakes and, if liked, crimp the edges with the fingers.

Makes 2 cakes

SOMERSET TREACLE CAKE

A wonderfully moist and spicy cake. Be prepared for the fruit to sink a little.

5 oz (150 g) self-raising flour	5 level tablespoons
1 teaspoon mixed spice	(6 oz/175 g) black treacle
4 oz (100 g) soft margarine	2 eggs
3 oz (75 g) caster sugar	4 oz (100 g) sultanas
	sieved icing sugar, for topping

Heat the oven to 325°F, 160°C, gas mark 3, and line a 7 inch (18 cm) square cake tin with greased greaseproof or silicone paper.

Using the all-in-one method, measure the flour, spice, soft margarine, caster sugar, black treacle, eggs and sultanas into one bowl and mix until all the ingredients are well blended. Turn the mixture into the prepared tin and level out the top.

Bake in the oven for about 1–1¼ hours until a skewer comes out clean when pushed into the centre of the cake. Turn on to a cooling tray.

To serve, dust the top with sieved icing sugar.

VERY SPECIAL MINCE PIE

A different and easier way of making mince pie. The attractive topping makes it less heavy, and as a bonus you get plenty of mincemeat in each slice!

Pastry Base
6 oz (175 g) flour
4 oz (100 g) block margarine
1 tablespoon icing sugar
2–3 tablespoons cold water

Topping
4 oz (100 g) margarine, just melted
4 oz (100 g) self-raising flour
2 oz (50 g) semolina
2 oz (50 g) caster sugar

Filling
about 1 lb (450 g) mincemeat

Lightly grease a 13 × 9 inch (33 × 23 cm) Swiss roll tin, and heat the oven to 400°F, 200°C, gas mark 6.

For the pastry base, measure the flour into a bowl and rub in the margarine until the mixture resembles fine breadcrumbs. Stir in the sugar and sufficient water to mix to a firm dough. Wrap in clear film and chill if time allows. Roll out on a lightly floured surface and use to line the tin. Spread generously with the mincemeat.

For the topping, measure all the ingredients into a bowl and knead together to form a soft dough. Using a coarse grater, grate this mixture on top of the mincemeat. If it is too soft to grate, then chill in the refrigerator for about 15 minutes.

Bake in the oven for about 40 minutes until pale golden brown. If it begins to get too brown then lay a piece of foil over the top. Allow to cool then serve in slices.

Serves 10 at least!

CUT AND COME AGAIN CAKE

A delicious family fruit cake which is always a favourite. If you like a milder flavour, use less mixed spice.

12 oz (350 g) self-raising flour
2 level teaspoons mixed spice
6 oz (175 g) soft margarine
6 oz (175 g) caster sugar
3 eggs

6 oz (175 g) currants
4 oz (100 g) raisins
4 oz (100 g) sultanas
3 tablespoons milk

Heat the oven to 350°F, 180°C, gas mark 4, and grease and line an 8 inch (20 cm) deep round cake tin with greased greaseproof paper.

Measure all the ingredients into a large bowl and beat well until thoroughly mixed. Turn into the prepared tin and level out evenly.

Bake in the oven for about 1¾ hours; a skewer should come out clean when pushed into the centre of the cake.

Leave to cool in the tin for about 10 minutes, then turn out, peel off paper and finish the cooling on a wire rack.

FIRST-RATE FAMILY FRUIT CAKE

Don't be tempted to be over-generous with the marmalade, otherwise the cake is likely to sink in the middle.

8 oz (225 g) soft margarine
8 oz (225 g) light muscovado
  sugar
12 oz (350 g) self-raising flour
3 oz (75 g) glacé cherries,
  quartered
1 lb (450 g) mixed dried fruit

2 level tablespoons
  marmalade
4 eggs

Topping
2 oz (50 g) flaked almonds

Lightly grease and line a 9 inch (23 cm) deep round cake tin with greased greaseproof paper. Heat the oven to 325°F, 160°C, gas mark 3.

Measure all the ingredients together into a bowl and mix well until blended. Turn into the tin and level out evenly. Sprinkle with the flaked almonds.

Bake in the oven for about 2¾ hours; pierce the cake in the centre with a skewer, which should come out clean.

Leave in the tin to cool for about 10 minutes, then turn out and finish cooling on a wire rack.

PINEAPPLE AND CHERRY CAKE

This is a really moist cake, and is best stored in the refrigerator and eaten within four weeks. The pineapple gives a very special flavour. Make sure to drain it thoroughly, and use the juice in a fruit salad. (You could use canned apricots instead of the pineapple if you liked.)

2 oz (50 g) glacé cherries
1 × 8 oz (225 g) can pineapple
  chunks, thoroughly drained
5 oz (150 g) soft margarine
5 oz (150 g) light muscovado
  sugar

2 large eggs, beaten
7 oz (200 g) self-raising flour
2 tablespoons milk
12 oz (350 g) mixed dried fruit

Heat the oven to 325°F, 160°C, gas mark 3. Grease and line a 7 inch (18 cm) deep square cake tin with greased greaseproof paper.

Cut the cherries in half, rinse under running cold water then dry thoroughly. Drain and chop the pineapple very finely.

Cream the margarine and sugar together in a bowl. Beat in the eggs a little at a time, adding 1 tablespoon flour with each addition of egg. Fold in the remaining flour, milk, dried fruit, cherries and pineapple. Turn the mixture into the prepared tin and level out evenly.

Bake in the oven for about 2 hours until pale golden brown and shrinking away from the sides of the tin. A fine skewer should come out clean when pushed into the cake.

Leave to cool in the tin, remove paper and store in a plastic container in the refrigerator.

If liked, decorate the top when cold with rows of blanched almonds, walnuts and hazelnuts, alternating with glacé cherries and topped with an apricot glaze.

DUNDEE CAKE

One of the great favourites. Be careful just to rest the almonds on top of the mixture before cooking so that they do not sink right into the cake mixture.

6 oz (175 g) soft margarine
5 oz (150 g) caster sugar
3 eggs
7 oz (200 g) self-raising flour
1 teaspoon baking powder
1 tablespoon sherry
1 tablespoon rum
1 oz (25 g) ground almonds
2 oz (50 g) mixed peel

4 oz (100 g) sultanas
4 oz (100 g) currants
4 oz (100 g) raisins
2 oz (50 g) glacé cherries, quartered

Topping
1 oz (25 g) split blanched almonds

Heat the oven to 300°F, 150°C, gas mark 2. Grease and line an 8 inch (20 cm) deep round cake tin with greased greaseproof paper.

Measure the margarine and sugar into a bowl and cream together until light and fluffy. Beat in the eggs a little at a time together with 2 tablespoons of the flour. Fold in the remaining flour with the remaining ingredients until evenly blended. Turn into the prepared tin and level the top.

Arrange the split almonds gently on top of the mixture then bake in the oven for about 2½–3 hours. To test that the cake is cooked, insert a fine skewer into the centre of the cake; if it comes out clean, the cake is cooked.

Allow to cool in the tin for about 30 minutes, then turn out and finish cooling on a wire rack.

PARADISE FRUIT CAKE

A rich fruit cake topped with cherries and nuts.

1 lb (450 g) mixed dried fruit	
3 tablespoons sherry	} soaked together overnight
grated rind and juice of 1 orange	

2 oz (50 g) glacé cherries, washed and dried

2 oz (50 g) walnuts

6 oz (175 g) soft margarine

5 oz (150 g) light muscovado sugar

9 oz (250 g) self-raising flour

2 level teaspoons ground mixed spice

4 eggs

1 level tablespoon apricot jam

1 level tablespoon treacle

Topping
apricot jam
halved glacé cherries
halved almonds

Grease and line an 8 inch (20 cm) deep round cake tin with greased greaseproof paper. Heat the oven to 300°F, 150°C, gas mark 2.

Measure all the ingredients for the cake into a large bowl and mix well until thoroughly blended. Turn into the prepared tin and level out evenly.

Bake in the oven for 2 hours, then at 275°F, 140°C, gas mark 1 for a further 1¼ hours. Test with a warm skewer: if it comes out clean then the cake is done. The top will be paler in colour than is usual.

Leave to cool in the tin then turn out and peel off paper.

To decorate, brush the top of the cake with apricot jam, arrange the cherries and nuts on top, and brush with more jam. Store in an airtight tin for up to 3 weeks.

OLD ENGLISH CHERRY CAKE

Do be sure to wash the cherries and then dry them thoroughly before adding to the mixture. This stops them from sinking to the bottom of the cake during baking.

8 oz (225 g) self-raising flour
1 teaspoon baking powder
6 oz (175 g) soft margarine
6 oz (175 g) caster sugar

3 eggs, beaten
4 oz (100 g) glacé cherries, quartered

Heat the oven to 325°F, 160°C, gas mark 3, and grease and line a 7 inch (18 cm) deep round cake tin with greased greaseproof paper.

Measure all the ingredients into a bowl and beat well until thoroughly blended. Turn the mixture into the prepared tin and level out evenly.

Bake in the oven for about 1½ hours or until a fine skewer pushed into the centre of the cake comes out clean.

Leave to cool in the tin for 5 minutes, then turn out, peel off paper and finish cooling on a wire rack.

RAISIN AND RUM CAKE

A light, moist cake using the all-in-one method. Remember to soak the raisins the night before.

1 lb (450 g) raisins
5 tablespoons rum
8 oz (225 g) soft margarine

8 oz (225 g) caster sugar
10 oz (275 g) self-raising flour
4 eggs, beaten

Soak the raisins in the rum overnight to plump them up and absorb the flavour.

Heat the oven to 325°F, 160°C, gas mark 3, and grease and line a 9 inch (23 cm) round cake tin with greased greaseproof paper.

Measure the margarine, sugar, flour and eggs into a large mixing bowl and beat well until thoroughly blended. Add the soaked raisins and mix until the fruit is evenly distributed. Spoon the mixture into the cake tin and level the top.

Bake in the oven for about 1½ hours until golden brown, well risen and firm to the touch.

Leave to cool in the tin for a few minutes then turn out on to a wire cooling rack.

BLACK FOREST GÂTEAU

Always a top favourite, and well worth the luxury of plenty of cream and cherry filling. Makes a wonderful dinner party pudding. Freezes well too.

4 eggs
4 oz (100 g) caster sugar
3 oz (75 g) self-raising flour
1 oz (25 g) cocoa, sieved

Filling and Topping
2 × 15 oz (420 g) cans stoned
   black cherries

2 level tablespoons cornflour
4 tablespoons Kirsch
¾ pint (450 ml) whipping
   cream, whipped
grated chocolate or chocolate
   curls

Heat the oven to 400°F, 200°C, gas mark 6 and grease and line two 9 inch (23 cm) sandwich tins with greased greaseproof paper.

Break the eggs into a mixing bowl, add the sugar and whisk with an electric whisk until the mixture is thick enough to leave a faint trail when lifted out of the bowl. Fold in the sieved flour and cocoa, using a metal spoon, then divide the mixture carefully between the tins.

Bake in the oven for about 20–25 minutes until the sponges are well risen and beginning to shrink away from the sides of the tins. Turn on to a wire rack to cool.

Drain the cans of cherries and save the juice. Keep a few cherries on one side for decorating the top of the gâteau. Place the cornflour in a small saucepan and stir in the cherry juice over a moderate heat. Bring to the boil, stirring until thickened, simmer for 2 minutes, then remove from the heat and cool. Add the Kirsch and cherries to the sauce.

Cut each sponge in half with a long, sharp knife so that you have four layers. Sandwich the sponges together with the whipped cream and cherry mixture. Spread cream thinly around the sides of the cake and coat with the grated chocolate or chocolate curls. Spread the top with the remaining cream and decorate with the reserved cherries and more chocolate.

Serves 10–12

Cakes for Desserts

One of the great advantages of nearly all the cake recipes in this section is that they can be made ahead – a boon when you're preparing other courses for a family or more formal meal.

The meringue cakes can be made several days in advance and should be stored carefully in polythene bags in an airtight tin. It's best to make pavlovas on the day, or only a day ahead. Assemble both meringues and pavlovas with their fillings and decorations when needed.

Pastry flan cases can be made ahead too, then filled an hour or so before serving. Cheesecakes and crumb flan cases can be made up in advance, and they freeze well.

Dessert cakes can be accompanied by whipped cream, old-fashioned home-made custard, or a special sauce, whichever is appropriate. They can be decorated attractively with cream or, best, with some fresh fruit. I occasionally decorate dessert cakes with crystallized grapes: simply brush grapes with egg white, dip in caster sugar and leave until dry.

There are many other cakes throughout the book which could be served as dessert, in the chocolate and continental sections particularly.

RASPBERRY MERINGUE BASKET

The secret of making meringues is simple: use an electric whisk, whisk egg whites until stiff and then add the sugar to the whites little by little, whisking all the time until the sugar is incorporated.

3 egg whites
6 oz (175 g) caster sugar

Filling
½ pint (300 ml) whipping cream
12 oz (350 g) fresh raspberries

Line a baking tray with silicone paper, and mark an 8 inch (20 cm) circle. Heat the oven to 225°F, 110°C, gas mark ¼ .

Put the egg whites in a large bowl and whisk until they form soft peaks. With the whisk still on full speed, add the sugar a teaspoonful at a time, whisking well after each addition. Spoon the mixture into a piping bag fitted with a large rose pipe, or star nozzle, and fill the centre of the circle with the meringue to make a flat base. Pipe rosettes of meringue around the edge to build up the sides and form a basket.

Bake in the oven for 3–4 hours or until the meringue is crisp and has dried out thoroughly. Remove from the oven and leave to cool completely then carefully peel off the paper.

An hour before serving, lightly whip the cream and fold in half the raspberries. Pile the mixture into the basket and decorate with the remaining fruit.

Serves 6

PEAR AND GINGER MERINGUE

This really is a spectacular dessert cake. The meringues can be made well ahead and stored in an airtight container. Such a good way of using up the stem ginger left in the jar after Christmas.

4 egg whites
8 oz (225 g) caster sugar

Filling
½ pint (300 ml) double cream

1 oz (25 g) caster sugar
1 × 14 oz (397 g) can pear
   halves, drained thoroughly
4 oz (100 g) stem ginger

Line two large baking trays with silicone paper. On one paper mark out a circle 8 inches (20 cm) in diameter. On the other mark one circle 7 inches (18 cm) and another 5 inches (13 cm) in diameter. Use plates and saucers as guides. Heat the oven to 225°F, 110°C, gas mark ¼ .

To make the meringue cases, whisk the egg whites until they form soft peaks. Then add the sugar in teaspoonfuls, whisking the mixture well after each addition. Continue until all but 3 teaspoons of sugar has been incorporated.

Divide the mixture among the marked circles, spreading it out to cover them evenly. On the smallest one, lift up the meringue in peaks then sprinkle it with the remaining sugar. Bake in the oven for about 3–4 hours until firm and an off-white colour. When the meringue layers are completely firm to the touch remove from the oven, leave to cool then peel off the paper.

To serve, lightly whip the cream, and add the sugar. Chop the pears and ginger and fold into the cream. Spread a generous half of this mixture on the largest circle, the rest on the second largest, then assemble the cake in layers on a serving plate. The cake should be assembled about 45 minutes before serving, as this softens the meringue a little.

Serves 6

HAZELNUT MERINGUE CAKE

Meringue and hazelnuts is a delicious combination. Leave to stand for at least 4 hours before serving.

4 oz (100 g) hazelnuts	*Filling*
4 egg whites	½ pint (300 ml) whipping
8 oz (225 g) caster sugar	cream
1 teaspoon white wine vinegar	2 tablespoons brandy

Heat the oven to 350°F, 180°C, gas mark 4. Lightly brush the sides of two 8 inch (20 cm) sandwich tins with oil, and line the bases with non-stick silicone paper.

Place the hazelnuts on a baking tray and put in the oven for about 10 minutes, then tip on to a clean tea towel. Rub well together to remove all the skins. Place in a processor or blender and grind.

Whisk the egg whites on maximum speed with an electric whisk until stiff then whisk in the sugar a teaspoonful at a time. Carefully fold in the ground hazelnuts with the vinegar.

Divide the mixture between the two sandwich tins and level out evenly. Bake in the oven for 45 minutes then turn off the heat and leave to cool in the oven. Turn out of the tins and peel off the paper.

Place one meringue on a serving plate. Lightly whip the cream until thick, then stir in the brandy and use to sandwich the two meringues together.

Serves 8

BABY MERINGUES WITH BUTTER CARAMEL SAUCE

Terribly wicked and extravagant, but absolutely delicious, this is a real treat for a special occasion. The sauce is also good as a topping for ice creams.

4 egg whites
8 oz (225 g) caster sugar

Sauce
3 oz (75 g) butter
5 oz (150 g) golden granulated
  sugar
1 × 6 oz (175 g) can
  evaporated milk

Filling
½ pint (300 ml) whipping
  cream, whipped

Heat the oven to 225°F, 110°C, gas mark ¼ . Line two baking trays with silicone paper.

Put the egg whites in a large clean bowl and whisk with an electric whisk on full speed until they form soft peaks. Add the sugar a teaspoonful at a time, whisking well after each addition, until all the sugar has been added. Put the mixture into a piping bag fitted with a ½ inch (1 cm) plain icing nozzle and pipe about 50 small blobs on the baking trays.

Bake in the oven for 2–3 hours until the meringues are firm and dry and lift easily from the tray.

Meanwhile prepare the sauce. Measure all the ingredients into a pan, and heat gently until the sugar has dissolved completely. Bring to the boil for about 5 minutes until pale golden and still runny. Allow to cool to a pouring consistency.

Sandwich the meringue shells together with the whipped cream and pile high on a serving plate. Pour the sauce over just before serving.

Serves 12

MINI BAKED ALASKAS

Once assembled, these mini alaskas can be left in the freezer for up to three days before being browned in the oven to serve. For celebrations, serve with a sparkler in the top. You could, of course, use your own home-made Swiss roll (see page 68), but bought is much more convenient!

1 Swiss roll	3 egg whites
2 tablespoons sherry	6 oz (175 g) caster sugar
about 12 scoops raspberry ripple ice cream	

Heat the oven to 450°F, 230°C, gas mark 8.

Slice the Swiss roll into six slices and arrange well spaced apart on a baking tray. Sprinkle with sherry. Pile the ice cream on to each of the slices of Swiss roll, then put in the freezer whilst preparing the meringue.

Whisk the egg whites until stiff then whisk in the sugar a teaspoonful at a time until all is incorporated. Take the ice cream baking tray out of the freezer and quickly spread the meringue around each of the ice creams so they are completely sealed.

Bake in the oven for about 3 minutes until the meringue is tinged a pale golden brown. Serve immediately.

Serves 6

STRAWBERRY PAVLOVA

*Use raspberries or loganberries for a change, if you like, instead
of the strawberries, and it can also be transformed into a really
dreamy dessert cake for chocolate lovers as in the Chocolate
Pavlova.*

Pavlova
3 egg whites
6 oz (175 g) caster sugar
1 teaspoon cornflour
1 teaspoon white wine vinegar

Filling
8 oz (225 g) strawberries
½ pint (300 ml) whipping
   cream, whipped

Lay a sheet of silicone paper on a baking tray and mark an
8 inch (20 cm) circle on it. Heat the oven to 325°F, 160°C, gas
mark 3.

To make the pavlova, whisk the egg whites with an electric
whisk until stiff, then add the sugar a teaspoonful at a time,
whilst still whisking on full speed. Blend the cornflour and
vinegar together and whisk into the whites. Spread the
meringue out to cover the circle on the baking tray, building up
the sides so they are higher than the middle.

Put in the oven and immediately reduce the temperature to
300°F, 150°C, gas mark 2. Bake the pavlova for about an hour
until firm to the touch and a pale beige colour. Turn the oven
off and let the pavlova become quite cold in the oven.

Remove the pavlova from the baking tray and put on a serving
plate. Hull the strawberries then cut into quarters. Stir into the
whipped cream then pile this mixture into the pavlova. Leave
in the refrigerator for an hour before serving.

Serves 6–8

Chocolate Pavlova

Make up the pavlova as in the previous recipe, adding ½ oz (15 g) sieved cocoa with the cornflour and vinegar. Bake as in the previous recipe and leave to cool.

Fill with ½ pint (300 ml) whipped whipping cream, and serve with the following sauce.

Sauce
12 oz (350 g) light muscovado sugar
4 level tablespoons cocoa, sieved

4 oz (100g) butter
4 tablespoons golden syrup
¼ pint (150 ml) milk

Gently heat all the ingredients in a pan until the butter has melted and the sugar has dissolved. Boil rapidly for 2 minutes until syrupy. Serve warm with the pavlova.

RUM DESSERT CAKE

This is rich and very special. It is possible to split the sponge base soon after it has cooled. If preferred, fill the cake with ½ pint (300 ml) double cream, whipped with 3 tablespoons rum and a little caster sugar.

If you have 2 × 8 inch (20 cm) round sandwich tins you will find that they will cook quickly in about 25 minutes and of course you will only have to split each sandwich once to make the four layers. I have suggested using evaporated milk in the icing – this makes it richer – but ordinary milk works well too. If the thought of making chocolate curls daunts you, just decorate with chocolate flake or chocolate coffee beans.

4 eggs
4 oz (100 g) caster sugar
3 oz (75 g) self-raising flour
1 oz (25 g) cocoa, sieved
3 tablespoons sunflower oil

Icing
6 tablespoons evaporated milk
1 tablespoon rum
6 oz (175 g) plain chocolate,
   broken into small pieces

Filling
5 oz (150 g) soft margarine
8 oz (225 g) icing sugar, sieved
3 tablespoons rum

Decoration
Chocolate curls (see page 10)

Grease and line an 8 inch (20 cm) deep round cake tin with greased greaseproof paper. Heat the oven to 350°F, 180°C, gas mark 4.

Break the eggs into a bowl, add the sugar, and whisk until the mixture is light and creamy, and the whisk leaves a trail when it is lifted out. Gently fold in the flour and cocoa, then gently fold in the oil. Turn the mixture into the prepared tin.

Bake in the oven for about 45 minutes until well risen and the cake is shrinking away slightly from the side of the tin. Leave to cool in the tin for a few minutes, then lift out, peel off paper and finish cooling on a wire rack.

When completely cold, carefully split into four rounds.

For the filling, blend all the ingredients together in a bowl until smooth. Spread the three lower rounds of the cake with this and then re-stack them again.

For the icing, heat the evaporated milk and rum in a pan over a low heat until very hot but not boiling. Remove from the heat and add the chocolate. Stir until the chocolate has dissolved, returning the pan to a gentle heat if necessary. Allow the icing to cool, stirring from time to time, until it will just coat the back of the spoon. Pour the icing over the cake and leave to set. Decorate with chocolate curls.

Serves 8

GOOSEBERRY CAKE

A delicious pudding cake to serve warm with cream, ice cream or real custard.

8 oz (225 g) self-raising flour
1 level teaspoon baking
   powder
grated rind of 1 lemon
4 oz (100 g) light muscovado
   sugar
4 oz (100 g) block margarine,
   melted

1 egg, beaten
4 tablespoons milk
12 oz (350 g) gooseberries,
   topped and tailed

Topping
1 tablespoon demerara sugar

Heat the oven to 350°F, 180°C, gas mark 4. Lightly grease an 8 inch (20 cm) loose-bottomed round cake tin.

Measure all the ingredients, except the gooseberries, into a bowl and beat well until thoroughly blended. Spoon half of the mixture into the tin and level out. Top with the gooseberries, and then roughly spoon over the remaining mixture. Sprinkle over the demerara sugar.

Bake in the oven for about 1 hour 20 minutes, until golden brown and shrinking away from the sides of the tin slightly.

Allow to cool for a few moments then remove from the tin and serve warm.

Serves 6

TARTE TATIN

This tart has a wonderful crisp base as it is baked upside down.

2 oz (50 g) butter	*Pastry*
2 oz (50 g) light muscovado sugar	4 oz (100 g) flour
2 lb (900 g) Cox's dessert apples, peeled, cored and thickly sliced	3 oz (75 g) butter
	1 egg yolk
	a scant tablespoon water
finely grated rind and juice of 1 lemon	½ oz (15 g) icing sugar

Heat the oven to 425°F, 220°C, gas mark 7, and lightly grease an 8 inch (20 cm) sandwich tin.

Measure the butter and sugar into a heavy pan, and melt gently, without boiling, until the sugar has dissolved, stirring occasionally. Add the apples, lemon juice and rind to the sugar mixture. Stir to coat the apples, then turn into the sandwich tin. Either leave apple pieces as they are, or arrange in a circle. Leave to cool.

For the pastry, put the flour in a large bowl. Cut the butter into the flour and rub in with the fingertips until the mixture resembles fine breadcrumbs. Add the egg yolk, water and icing sugar and mix to a firm dough. Roll out on a lightly floured surface and use to cover the apples. Trim off surplus pastry.

Bake in the oven for 20–25 minutes, until the pastry is crisp and golden brown. When cooked take out of the oven: the pastry will have shrunk a little. Tip the juices from the tin into a small saucepan and reduce to a caramelized sauce for about 3–4 minutes. Turn the tart out on to a plate, with the pastry on the bottom, and pour the reduced sauce over the apples. Serve warm or cold with plenty of cream or plain yoghurt.

Serves 6

SPECIAL LEMON FLAN

A great favourite in our family. I used to make the filling with cream, which makes it richer, but now I use plain yoghurt instead. If you use an electric whisk for the sponge, there is no need to warm the sugar.

You can use the sponge flan as the base for other fillings. We like it filled with scoops of mint and chocolate chip ice cream, perhaps with a little whipped cream, and decorated with a few chocolate dessert mints.

Sponge Flan
2 eggs
2 oz (50 g) caster sugar, warmed
2 oz (50 g) self-raising flour

Lemon Filling
1 small can condensed milk

1 × 5 oz (150 g) carton plain yoghurt
finely grated rind and juice of 2 lemons

Topping
fresh fruit (grapes, raspberries or strawberries) to decorate

Grease an 8 inch (20 cm) sponge flan tin. Heat the oven to 375°F, 190°C, gas mark 5.

Break the eggs into a large bowl, add the sugar and whisk until thick, white and creamy: when the whisk is lifted out it should leave a trail in the mixture. Sieve in the flour a little at a time, folding in gently until smooth. Turn into the tin and level out.

Bake in the oven for about 20 minutes until pale golden and shrinking away from the sides of the tin. Leave to cool in the tin for a couple of minutes, then turn out on to a wire rack to finish cooling.

For the filling, whisk the condensed milk, yoghurt, lemon rind and juice together until smooth. Pour into the flan case and leave to set in the fridge for at least 3 hours or overnight.

To serve, decorate with fresh fruit.

Serves 6

PINEAPPLE TART

A rich shortbread case with a pineapple and custard filling, which is best served warm. For a change, try a can of apricot halves, chopped, in the middle.

Shortbread Case
6 oz (175 g) flour
2 oz (50 g) icing sugar
4 oz (100 g) butter

Filling
1 × 15 oz (432 g) can
    pineapple pieces in natural
    juice, well drained
4 eggs, beaten
3 oz (75 g) caster sugar
1 oz (25 g) butter, melted

Put a large baking tray in the oven, and heat the oven to 350°F, 180°C, gas mark 4.

For the shortbread, measure the flour and sugar into a bowl and rub in the butter until the mixture resembles fine breadcrumbs. Knead lightly together then press into a 9 inch (23 cm) loose-bottomed flan tin to evenly cover the base and sides. Chill in the refrigerator for about 15 minutes, then line with a piece of foil.

Bake on the hot baking tray for about 20 minutes until pale golden brown, removing the foil for the last 5 minutes.

For the filling, roughly chop the pineapple and spread over the base of the baked case. Blend the eggs, sugar and melted butter together in a bowl, then pour through a sieve on to the pineapple. Carefully return to the oven and bake for a further 30–35 minutes until pale golden brown and the filling has set.

Serve warm in slim wedges.

Serves 8

EXOTIC FRUIT TART

This tart looks stunning. It is essential to chill the pastry before baking, otherwise the sides of the pastry will slip down the sides of the flan tin during baking.

If you have no vanilla sugar, use ½ teaspoon of vanilla essence instead. For a lighter crème pâtissière use 1 whole egg and 1 yolk blended together instead of 3 yolks. The fruit topping can vary with the seasons – strawberries and kiwi fruits go well together. Choose even-sized large strawberries and slice them, arrange cut side down, or if you can get them use whole small strawberries. If no soft fruits are available use only black and green grapes. Choose the large ones, cut them in half and remove the pips then arrange in circles of black and green, and cover with the glaze.

The completed tart does not freeze well – it would be soggy on thawing. However, the pastry flan case freezes well, preferably uncooked in the tin and wrapped.

Pastry
6 oz (175 g) plain flour
4 oz (100 g) butter
1 egg yolk
1 tablespoon caster sugar
a scant 2 tablespoons cold
   water

Crème Pâtissière
3 egg yolks
3 oz (75 g) vanilla sugar (see
   page 9)
1 oz (25 g) flour
½ pint (300 ml) milk

Topping
2 kiwi fruit
8 oz (225 g) fresh raspberries
4 oz (100 g) seedless grapes,
   halved
1 teaspoon arrowroot
juice of ½ lemon
4 tablespoons water
2 teaspoons caster sugar
1 tablespoon brandy

For the pastry, put the flour in a bowl, add butter, and rub in until mixture resembles fine breadcrumbs. Mix the egg yolk, sugar and water together, then stir into the dry ingredients and bind. Roll out on a lightly floured surface and use to line a 9 inch (23 cm) flan tin. Chill for about 30 minutes.

Meanwhile, heat the oven to 425°F, 220°C, gas mark 7, and place a thick baking tray in it.

Line the flan with foil and bake blind on the hot baking tray for about 10 minutes until beginning to brown at the edges. Remove foil and cook for a further 5 minutes. Allow to cool in the tin then carefully lift on to a flat serving plate.

For the *crème pâtissière*, put the yolks, sugar and flour in a bowl with a little of the milk and mix to a smooth paste. Bring the rest of the milk to the boil then pour on to the egg yolk mixture, and whisk well. Return the mixture to the pan and heat gently until smooth and thickened. Leave to cool, stirring from time to time. Spread on the flan case.

Paradise Fruit Cake, Sharp Lemon Squares, Very Special Mince Pie

Pear and Ginger Meringue, Easy but Wonderful Lemon Cheesecake

Iced Chocolate Charlotte, Chocolate Swiss Roll, Chocolate Brownies

Scrumpy Teabread, Shortbread, American Orange Mega-Muffins

Apple Strüdel, Danish Pastries, Viennese Tea Cakes

Simple Royal Iced Christmas Cake

Chocolate Chip Cookies, Lemon Stars, Gingerbread Men, Caterpillar Cake

Treasure Trove Cake

Peel and slice the kiwi fruits and arrange on the top of the flan with the raspberries and halved grapes.

Put the arrowroot in a pan and blend with the lemon juice and water. Bring to the boil, and stir until smooth and thickened, a few minutes only. Stir in the sugar and brandy and then spoon over the top of the fruits to give a shiny glaze.

Serves 8

EASY BUT WONDERFUL LEMON CHEESECAKE

This cheesecake can be made in next to no time, and it can easily be adapted as in the variation below.

When making the bases for cheesecakes, don't always use digestive biscuits – try ginger or broken biscuits too. And to crush them, put in two paper bags and run over with a rolling pin. I often walk *on the bags!*

Crust
10 digestive biscuits, crushed
2 oz (50 g) butter, melted
1 tablespoon demerara sugar

Cheesecake
¼ pint (150 ml) single cream
1 small can condensed milk
4 oz (100 g) low-fat soft
   cheese, softened
grated rind and juice of 2
   large lemons

Topping
¼ pint (150 ml) whipping
   cream, whipped
a few fresh strawberries or
   grapes

Measure all the ingredients for the crust into a bowl and mix well. Turn into an 8 inch (20 cm) flan dish and press evenly over the base and sides. Leave to set.

For the filling, mix together the cream, condensed milk, soft cheese and lemon rind, then beat in the lemon juice a little at a time. Pour the mixture into the flan case and leave to chill in the refrigerator for 3–4 hours, or overnight.

To serve, decorate with swirls of cream and a few fresh strawberries or grapes.

Serves 6

Summer Fruit Cheesecake Slices

The crust and filling are made in exactly the same way as in the previous recipe, but in a 7 inch (18 cm) square cake tin lined with clear film. Leave it overnight before adding the following topping.

Topping	4 teaspoons arrowroot
8 oz (225 g) frozen summer fruits, thawed	1 tablespoon water
2 tablespoons sugar	

For the topping, put the fruits and sugar into a pan and heat gently to dissolve the sugar. Blend the arrowroot with the water and add to the pan. Stir gently until thickened then remove from the heat. Do not overcook otherwise the fruit will become mushy. Leave to cool.

To assemble, carefully lift the cheesecake out of the tin, using the clear film. Divide in half then stand on a long serving plate end to end. Spoon over the fruits then chill in the fridge before serving.

Serves 10

CHILLED CHEESECAKE

*This is a very special lemon cheesecake. The strawberry and
cream topping makes it particularly delicious to serve as a
midsummer treat.*

Crust
10 digestive biscuits, crushed
1 oz (25 g) demerara sugar
2 oz (50 g) butter, melted

Cheesecake
½ oz (15 g) powdered gelatine
4 tablespoons cold water
finely grated rind and juice of
   2 large lemons
3 eggs, separated

4 oz (100 g) caster sugar
½ pint (300 ml) whipping
   cream, lightly whipped
12 oz (350 g) low-fat cream
   cheese, softened

Decoration
4 oz (100 g) fresh small
   strawberries

Measure all the ingredients for the crust into a bowl and mix
well. Press on to the base of a deep 8 inch (20 cm) loose-
bottomed cake tin, and leave to set.

For the filling, put the gelatine in a small bowl with the water
and leave to stand for about 5 minutes to form a sponge. Stand
over a pan of simmering water until clear and dissolved.

Put the lemon juice and rind, egg yolks and sugar in a large
bowl and whisk with an electric whisk until thick and foamy.
Blend in the cooled gelatine, cream (saving 2 tablespoons for
decoration), and softened cheese. Whisk the egg whites until
they form soft peaks then fold into the mixture. Turn into the
prepared tin and level out evenly. Chill in the refrigerator until
it has set.

To serve, carefully remove from the tin and transfer to a
serving plate. Decorate with the remaining whipped cream and
top with the halved strawberries.

Serves 6–8

GINGER GRAPEFRUIT CHEESECAKE

The biscuit crust is put on top of the cheesecake so that when it is turned out it is really crisp underneath. This cheesecake freezes well.

Cheesecake
½ oz (15 g) gelatine
3 tablespoons cold water
1 lb (450 g) rich cream cheese
6 oz (175 g) unsweetened
  frozen grapefruit juice,
  thawed
3 oz (75 g) caster sugar
½ pint (300 ml) whipping
  cream, whipped

Base
4 oz (100 g) ginger biscuits,
  crushed
2 oz (50 g) butter, melted
1 oz (25 g) demerara sugar

Decoration
a few strawberries and
  whipped cream

First oil an 8 inch (20 cm) shallow cake tin, then line with an oiled disc of greaseproof paper.

For the cheesecake, put the gelatine in a small bowl, add water and leave to form a sponge. Stand the bowl in hot water until dissolved. Cool a little.

Measure all the other ingredients, except the cream, into a processor, add the cool but not set gelatine, and process until smooth. Add the cream, and process for a moment until blended. (If you haven't a processor, beat cheese, juice, sugar and dissolved gelatine until smooth, then fold in the cream.) Pour into the prepared tin and chill until set.

Mix the ingredients for the crust together, cool, then spoon over the cheesecake. Chill until firm in the refrigerator.

To turn out, loosen the sides then put a flat serving plate on top of the tin and turn the cheesecake on to the plate. Remove greaseproof paper. Decorate with strawberries and whipped cream.

Serves 8

GINGER CREAM ROLL

I make no apology for the simplicity of this recipe – it is a real cheat but so delicious!

¾ pint (450 ml) whipping
  cream
1 × 8 oz (225 g) packet ginger
  biscuits

Decoration
stem ginger

Measure half the cream into a bowl and whisk until it forms fairly stiff peaks. Use it to sandwich the biscuits together in a long roll.

Arrange the roll on a serving plate, cover and chill in the refrigerator overnight.

The next day, whip the remaining cream and use it to cover the ginger biscuit roll completely. Decorate the roll with small pieces of stem ginger. Cut diagonal pieces from the loaf shape or cut in slices.

Serves 6–8

Chocolate Cakes

Chocolate has been proved to be the world's favourite flavouring, and there are some people so enthusiastic that they're called chocoholics! Chocolate cakes are undeniably delicious, but they're also fattening, I'm afraid. However, an occasional treat never did anyone any harm.

Always use the best chocolate flavouring for cakes; I've defined my favourites on page 10. Block chocolate melts in a child's pocket or on a sunny windowsill, so it needs very little heat. This is why any melting must be done gently and very slowly. Break it into small pieces and put it in a bowl or handleless cup in a pan of hot water. You must never put chocolate over intense heat.

Chocolate cakes – and other cakes too – can be decorated with chocolate. You can use caraque or curls (see page 10), or, if time is short, grated chocolate, Maltesers, Treets or chocolate raisins make good finishing touches.

Other recipes for chocoholics appear throughout the book – for example, Black Forest Gâteau on page 38. Look in the children's section, for a few.

CHOCOLATE FUDGE CAKE

A wonderfully easy chocolate cake, which keeps well, too. The baked cakes freeze best unfilled and un-iced. Place a piece of greaseproof paper between them, wrap in foil then label and freeze. The icing is very untemperamental: make it ahead if it suits you, and just warm it enough to use.

2 eggs
¼ pint (150 ml) sunflower oil
¼ pint (150 ml) milk
2 tablespoons golden syrup
5 oz (150 g) caster sugar
6½ oz (190 g) self-raising
    flour
1 oz (25 g) cocoa, sieved
1 level teaspoon baking
    powder
1 level teaspoon bicarbonate
    of soda

Fudge Icing
2 oz (50 g) margarine
1 oz (25 g) cocoa, sieved
about 3 tablespoons milk
8 oz (225 g) icing sugar, sieved

To Finish
a little warmed apricot jam
chocolate flake or beans

Grease and line two 8 inch (20 cm) sandwich tins. Heat the oven to 325°F, 160°C, gas mark 3.

Break the eggs into a large mixing bowl, add the remaining cake ingredients and beat well for about 2 minutes, until thoroughly mixed. Divide between the two tins.

Bake in the oven for about 30–35 minutes until the cakes spring back when lightly pressed with a finger and are shrinking away slightly from the sides of the tin. Turn out on to a wire rack to cool. Peel off paper.

For the icing, melt the margarine in a pan, add the cocoa and cook for a minute, then remove from the heat and stir in the milk and icing sugar. Beat well until smooth. Cool until a spreading consistency.

Spread the *underneath* of one cake with apricot jam. If there are a few pieces of apricot make sure they are in the middle of the cake. Place on a plate, top down, apricot side up. Spread this side with half the chocolate icing, then put the bottom of the second cake on top – so bottom to bottom. Spread the top of the sandwiched cake with jam, then pour the remainder of the chocolate icing over the top. If a little too thick, warm again in the pan first.

Decorate with some chocolate flake or groups of chocolate beans.

SICILIAN CAKE

A very simple plain cake, which is lovely to make for a weekend. It is very light in colour, but the combination of cocoa and almonds is an unusual one, I think.

2 oz (50 g) cocoa, sieved
4 tablespoons boiling water
6 oz (175 g) soft margarine
6 oz (175 g) caster sugar
3 eggs
3 oz (75 g) self-raising flour

3 oz (75 g) ground almonds
1 teaspoon baking powder

Topping
1 oz (25 g) split blanched
   almonds

Heat the oven to 325°F, 160°C, gas mark 3. Grease and line a 7 inch (18 cm) square cake tin with greased greaseproof paper.

Measure the cocoa into a bowl and mix to a smooth paste with the boiling water. Allow to cool, then add the remaining ingredients for the cake and beat well until thoroughly mixed. Turn into the prepared tin, level out evenly, and arrange the almonds on top.

Bake in the oven for about 1 hour or until the top of the cake springs back when lightly pressed with a finger.

Leave to cool in the tin for a few minutes, then turn out, peel off paper and finish cooling on a wire rack.

FRENCH CHOCOLATE GÂTEAU

Rich and special, this chocolate sponge is filled with real chocolate butter cream.

2 oz (50 g) plain chocolate,
  broken into small pieces
3 tablespoons water
3 eggs
4 oz (100 g) caster sugar
3 oz (75 g) self-raising flour

Butter Cream
2 oz (50 g) butter, softened
4 oz (100 g) icing sugar, sieved
2 oz (50 g) plain chocolate,
  melted

Decoration
2 oz (50 g) chocolate curls (see
  page 10)
a little icing sugar, to dust

Heat the oven to 350°F, 180°C, gas mark 4. Grease and line a 9 inch (23 cm) deep round cake tin with greased greaseproof paper.

Put the chocolate in a small pan, add the water and heat very gently until the chocolate has melted. Remove from the heat and cool.

Break the eggs into a bowl, add the sugar and whisk until thick and pale; the whisk should leave a trail when lifted out. Gently fold in the flour and cooled chocolate mixture until thoroughly blended. Turn into the prepared tin.

Bake in the oven for about 35 minutes. The cake should be shrinking slightly from the sides of the tin and spring back when lightly pressed with a finger. Allow to cool in the tin for a few moments, then turn out, peel off the paper and finish cooling on a wire rack.

For the butter cream, measure all the ingredients into a bowl and beat until smooth. When the cake is cold, split into two halves and sandwich together with a thin layer of butter cream. Spread the remaining butter cream evenly over the top and sides. Press the chocolate curls all over the cake, then sprinkle lightly with icing sugar.

CHOCOLATE SWISS ROLL

A basic recipe, but one that is an old favourite and always enjoyed. It's good used for Christmas log cake too (see page 128), and can be varied as on page 69.

3 eggs	*Filling*
3 oz (75 g) caster sugar	2 tablespoons strawberry jam
2 oz (50 g) self-raising flour	½ pint (300 ml) whipping
1 oz (25 g) cocoa, sieved	cream, whipped
a little caster sugar, to dredge	

Heat the oven to 425°F, 220°C, gas mark 7. Grease and line a 13 × 9 inch (33 × 23 cm) Swiss roll tin with greased greaseproof paper.

Break the eggs into a bowl, add the sugar and whisk with an electric whisk until thick and creamy; the whisk should leave a trail when it is lifted out of the mixture. Sieve the flour and cocoa into the mixture and very gently fold in with a metal spoon until thoroughly blended. Turn into the prepared tin and level out into the corners.

Bake in the oven for about 12 minutes until well risen and it springs back when lightly pressed with a finger.

Whilst the Swiss roll is baking, lay a sheet of greaseproof paper out on the work surface and sprinkle with caster sugar. Turn the Swiss roll out on to the sugared paper and peel off the cooking paper from underneath. Turn the paper so that the short side of the cake is towards you.

Trim the edges of the Swiss roll and make a score mark about 1 inch (2.5 cm) in from the front edge. Lay a clean sheet of greaseproof paper on top and roll up with the paper in the middle, folding the score mark in first to help with the rolling up. Allow to cool.

Carefully unroll the Swiss roll, remove the paper and spread first with a layer of strawberry jam, then cream. Carefully re-roll, and lift on to a serving plate.

Lemon Swiss Roll

For a plain lemon Swiss roll, omit the cocoa and use 3 oz (75 g) self-raising flour instead of 2 oz (50 g), and add the finely grated rind of a lemon. Fill with about 4 tablespoons lemon curd.

CHOCOLATE ROULADE WITH BRANDY CREAM

A truly delicious pudding cake. Don't worry that the sponge cracks as you roll it – it is meant to!

6 oz (175 g) plain chocolate, broken into small pieces
6 oz (175 g) caster sugar
6 eggs, separated

Filling
2 tablespoons brandy
½ pint (300 ml) double cream, whipped
icing sugar

Heat the oven to 350°F, 180°C, gas mark 4, and grease and line a 13 × 9 inch (33 × 23 cm) Swiss roll tin with greased greaseproof paper.

Put the chocolate into a bowl and stand over a pan of hot water to melt.

Measure the sugar and egg yolks into a bowl and whisk with an electric whisk on full speed until light and creamy. Carefully stir in the melted chocolate until blended.

Whisk the egg whites in a separate bowl until stiff, then fold gently into the chocolate mixture. Turn into the prepared tin and spread into the corners. Bake in the oven for about 20 minutes until firm to the touch.

Remove from the oven, leave in the tin and cover with a piece of greaseproof paper which has been wrung out with warm water. This paper should not actually be touching the top of the cake. Leave to stand for several hours or overnight.

Stir the brandy into the whipped cream. Dust a large sheet of greaseproof paper with icing sugar, turn out the roulade and peel off the paper. Spread with the cream and roll up like a Swiss roll, using the paper to help. Dust with icing sugar and place on a serving dish.

Serves 6–8

CHOCOLATE BROWNIES

American brownies are extremely sweet. This version uses less sugar than the Americans would use, and is one that my family enjoys.

1½ oz (40 g) cocoa, sieved
3 tablespoons boiling water
4 oz (100 g) soft margarine
5 oz (150 g) light muscovado
    sugar
2 eggs
4 oz (100 g) self-raising flour
1 teaspoon baking powder
2 oz (50 g) walnuts, chopped

Fudge Icing
1½ oz (40 g) block margarine
1 oz (25 g) cocoa, sieved
about 3 tablespoons milk
4 oz (100 g) icing sugar,
    sieved

Heat the oven to 375°F, 190°C, gas mark 5, and grease and line a 7 inch (18 cm) square tin with greased greaseproof paper.

Measure the cocoa into a bowl, add the boiling water and mix to a smooth paste. Add the margarine, sugar, eggs, flour, baking powder and walnuts and beat well until thoroughly mixed. Turn into the prepared tin and level out evenly.

Bake in the oven for about 30 minutes or until the centre of the cake springs back when lightly pressed with a finger. Leave to cool in the tin for a few moments, then turn out, peel off paper and finish cooling on a wire rack.

For the icing, heat the margarine in a small pan, stir in the cocoa and cook for a minute. Remove from the heat and stir in the milk and icing sugar. Mix well until a spreading consistency. Spread icing over the cake and leave to set. Serve cut in squares.

Makes 9 squares

CHOCOLATE ÉCLAIRS

People are often worried about choux pastry, but if you follow the instructions carefully, it will always work! Choux can, of course, be made into other shapes – profiteroles, or larger puffs, or religieuses, a cottage-loaf-shaped puff confection.

The choux pastry can be made most satisfactorily in a food processor. Measure the butter and water into a pan and boil as in the recipe. Put the flour and eggs in the processor, whizz for a few moments until smooth, then pour in the boiling liquid through the funnel as the flour and eggs are being processed. Continue until the mixture forms a smooth shiny firm paste – it takes a few moments.

If you like the centre of the éclair really dry, return to the oven after splitting the side of each éclair to let the steam out. Lowering the oven to 350°F, 180°C, gas mark 3, cook until the centre is dry – about a further 10 minutes. Then leave to cool. The icing is particularly good, it stays really shiny and is wonderful to eat. You might find it easier to spoon the icing over the éclairs if you don't have a suitable shallow dish to contain it.

Choux Pastry
2 oz (50 g) butter
¼ pint (150 ml) water
2½ oz (65 g) flour, sieved
2 eggs, beaten

Filling
½ pint (300 ml) whipping
   cream, whipped

Icing
2 oz (50 g) plain chocolate,
   broken into small pieces
2 tablespoons water
½ oz (15 g) butter
3 oz (75 g) icing sugar, sieved

Heat the oven to 425°F, 220°C, gas mark 7. Lightly grease a large baking tray.

For the choux pastry, measure the butter and water into a small pan, bring slowly to the boil and allow the butter to melt.

Remove from the heat, add the flour all at once, and beat until it forms a soft ball.

Gradually beat in the eggs, a little at a time, to give a smooth shiny paste.

Turn the mixture into a piping bag fitted with a ½ inch (1 cm) plain nozzle and pipe into 12 éclair shapes, about 5–6 inches (13–15 cm) long, leaving room for them to spread.

Bake in the oven for about 10 minutes then reduce the heat to 375°F, 190°C, gas mark 5. Cook for a further 20 minutes until well risen and golden brown. Remove from the oven and split one side of each éclair to allow the steam to escape. Cool on a wire rack.

Fill each of the éclairs with a little cream then, for the icing, measure the chocolate, water and butter into a bowl. Heat over a pan of simmering water until the chocolate and butter have melted. Remove from the heat and beat in the sugar until smooth. Pour into a shallow dish then dip each éclair into the icing to coat the top. Allow to set.

Makes 12 éclairs

CHOCOLATE CUPCAKES

Rich and irresistible, I find these easiest to ice whilst still in the bun tins.

1 rounded tablespoon cocoa,
   sieved
2 tablespoons hot water
4 oz (100 g) soft margarine
1 level teaspoon baking
   powder
6 oz (175 g) self-raising flour
6 oz (175 g) caster sugar
2 eggs
4 tablespoons milk

Icing
4 oz (100 g) plain chocolate,
   broken into small pieces
4 tablespoons hot water
1 oz (25 g) butter
6 oz (175 g) icing sugar,
   sieved

Heat the oven to 350°F, 180°C, gas mark 4. Use about 32 paper cases to line bun tins.

Measure the cocoa into a bowl and blend to a smooth paste with the hot water. Add the remaining ingredients and beat well until thoroughly blended.

Divide the mixture between the paper cases and bake in the oven for about 15–20 minutes until well risen. Allow to cool in the tins.

For the icing, measure the chocolate, water and butter into a bowl and heat over a pan of simmering water until the chocolate and butter have melted. Remove from the heat, stir in the icing sugar, and beat well until smooth. Pour a thin layer of the icing on top of each of the cakes and leave to set before lifting the cases out of the tins.

Makes about 32

CHOCOLATE MERINGUE SLICES

An oblong meringue cake which just melts in the mouth. Both the shape and the 'softening' time make the cake much easier to slice than conventional meringue circles. Make the meringues a week ahead if this suits you. Wrap in foil until you need to fill them.

4 egg whites
8 oz (225 g) caster sugar

Filling
½ pint (300 ml) double cream, whipped

Topping
1½ oz (40 g) soft margarine
1 oz (25 g) cocoa, sieved
2 tablespoons milk
4 oz (100 g) icing sugar, sieved
2 oz (50 g) plain chocolate, broken into small pieces

Heat the oven to 225°F, 110°C, gas mark ¼. Line two large baking trays with non-stick silicone paper.

Whisk the egg whites until stiff and gradually whisk in the sugar, a teaspoonful at a time, with the whisk still on full speed, until really stiff. Spread the meringue mixture into four oblongs about 12 × 4 inches (30 cm × 10 cm) and bake for about 3 hours until firm and a pale cream colour.

For the topping, heat the margarine in a small pan, stir in the cocoa and cook for a minute. Remove from the heat and stir in the milk and icing sugar. Beat until smooth and leave to cool until a spreading consistency.

Spread the chocolate topping over two of the meringues, on the rough side. Turn over the two remaining oblongs and spread the whipped cream on the flat sides. Sandwich the chocolate and cream pieces together, to give two cakes.

Melt the chocolate in a bowl over a pan of hot water, then turn into a polythene bag. Snip one corner off the bag to give a small hole, and drizzle the chocolate in a zig-zag pattern over the meringue. Leave for at least 4 hours for the meringue to soften, then serve in slices.

Each cake serves 6, so both will serve 12

ICED CHOCOLATE CHARLOTTE

A delicious and extravagant special dessert cake for those times when you need something quick but impressive. It's a good way of using up egg yolks after you've been making meringues.

4 oz (100 g) butter
4 oz (100 g) caster sugar
8 oz (225 g) plain chocolate,
   melted
3 egg yolks
2 tablespoons rum or brandy
½ pint (300 ml) whipping
   cream, whipped

To Serve
½ pint (300 ml) whipping
   cream, whipped
about 20 *langue de chat*
   biscuits
a few toasted flaked almonds

Line a 7 inch (18 cm) cake tin with clear film.

Put the butter, sugar, melted chocolate, egg yolks and rum or brandy into the processor and process until thoroughly blended. Fold this mixture into the whipped cream until evenly blended.

Turn into the cake tin, level out evenly and put in the freezer until firm.

Take the charlotte out of the freezer about an hour before serving. Peel off the clear film and stand on a serving plate. Spread cream thinly round the outside and stand the biscuits around the outside so they are just touching. Spread the remaining cream on top and fork into rough peaks, then sprinkle with a few toasted almonds.

Serves 8

FRESH CREAM RUM CHOCOLATE TRUFFLES

Wonderful with coffee after a special meal. Make a day ahead and keep in the fridge.

1 rounded tablespoon golden
 syrup
2 oz (50 g) cocoa, sieved
2 oz (50 g) butter
2 tablespoons double cream

4 tablespoons rum
12 oz (350 g) icing sugar,
 sieved
chocolate vermicelli, cocoa or
 drinking chocolate powder

Measure the syrup, cocoa, butter and cream into a pan. Stir at first over a low heat until well blended, then bring to the boil. Remove from the heat, add the rum and stir in the icing sugar. Beat until smooth, then chill well.

Roll into small balls, and toss in chocolate vermicelli, cocoa or drinking chocolate powder. Place each in a tiny paper case, and store in the refrigerator.

Makes about 60 truffles

Biscuits and Teabreads

Good home-made biscuits are delicious, I think, and very useful as they last well in airtight tins, and transport well for a lunchbox or picnic. There's a good selection here from which to choose.

Teabreads and fruit loaves are easy to make and they keep well. Spread with a little butter, they're ideal fare for hungry mouths at tea time.

Biscuits and teabreads are nice to give as presents to your hosts instead of a box of chocolates or bunch of flowers. Wrapped nicely in cellophane with a colourful ribbon perhaps, they would be very welcome. They'd also be much appreciated by those who haven't time to bake themselves, or someone, old or young, who lives on their own.

Many of the recipes here are suitable for selling at coffee mornings, the mincemeat fruit loaves particularly, as they're so easy to slice.

GINGER SHORTBREAD STREUSEL

A really good shortbread with an interesting squiggly finish. To make sure that the shortbread is cooked underneath, just take a small slice from one corner.

2 level teaspoons ground
   ginger
4 oz (100 g) caster sugar
8 oz (225 g) butter or
   margarine

8 oz (225 g) plain flour
4 oz (100 g) semolina or
   ground rice
a little demerara sugar

Heat the oven to 325°F, 160°C, gas mark 3, and have ready a 13 × 9 inch (33 × 23 cm) Swiss roll tin.

Measure all the ingredients, except the demerara sugar, into a processor or mixer, and process until just worked together. Divide the mixture in half and press out one half in a thin layer in the Swiss roll tin, using wet hands. Level out with a palette knife.

Grate the remaining mixture over the top with a coarse grater, then bake in the oven for about an hour until a pale golden colour.

Sprinkle with demerara sugar. Mark into 24 pieces then leave to cool in the tin for about 10 minutes. Lift out and finish cooling on a wire rack. Store in an airtight tin.

Makes 24 pieces

A REALLY GOOD SHORTBREAD

A good shortbread is an even, pale, biscuity beige colour – lift it up gently to see if it's the same colour underneath. Shortbread is always popular, and is handy to prepare for a bazaar, bring-and-buy sale, coffee morning, tea time or picnic.

The recipe can be varied slightly in a number of ways. You can use cornflour, ground rice or semolina, each of which gives slightly different textures; the cornflour is the least, the semolina the most, crunchy. You can make it in a square tin for fingers, or roll out to a circle for wedge-shaped petticoat tails.

4 oz (100 g) plain flour	2 oz (50 g) caster sugar
2 oz (50 g) cornflour, ground rice or semolina	a little caster sugar, for dusting
4 oz (100 g) butter	

Heat the oven to 325°F, 160°C, gas mark 3, and grease a 7 inch (18 cm) shallow square tin.

Mix the flour with the cornflour, ground rice or semolina into a bowl or food processor. Add butter and sugar. Rub together with fingertips or process, until the mixture is just beginning to bind together. Knead lightly, just until the dough forms a smooth ball.

Press the mixture into the tin and bake in the oven for about 35 minutes, or until a very pale golden brown.

Remove from the oven and mark into 12 fingers. Leave the shortbread to cool in the tin. Sprinkle with caster sugar.

Makes 12 fingers

Almond Shortbread

Prepare exactly as above but before putting in the oven, sprinkle the top with 1 oz (25 g) flaked almonds.

Petticoat Tails

Prepare exactly as above, but flatten the dough on to a greased baking tray and roll out to a 7 inch (18 cm) circle. Crimp the edges, prick all over with a fork, and mark into eight wedges. Chill until firm (it'll still spread slightly while baking).

Bake as in the basic shortbread above, then re-mark the sections, sprinkle with sugar and leave to cool on the baking tray for about 5 minutes. Lift off carefully with a palette knife, and finish cooling on a wire rack. Store in an airtight tin.

CRACKERJACKS

Good to have in the biscuit tin for everyday, and they're perfect to serve with coffee.

5 oz (150 g) soft margarine
1 rounded tablespoon golden
  syrup
3 oz (75 g) self-raising flour

6 oz (175 g) golden granulated
  sugar
3 oz (75 g) desiccated coconut
4 oz (100 g) porridge oats

Heat the oven to 350°F, 180°C, gas mark 4, and lightly grease two baking trays.

Measure the margarine and syrup into a pan, heat gently until melted, then stir in the remaining ingredients. Mix well until blended. Spoon about 36 slightly flattened mounds well apart on the trays.

Bake in the oven for about 10 minutes, until they have spread out flat and are lightly browned at the edges. Leave to cool on the trays for a few moments, then carefully lift off with a palette knife and finish cooling on a wire rack.

Makes about 36

GOLDEN CRUNCH COOKIES

These are really excellent home-made biscuits. Children enjoy making these themselves.

8 oz (225 g) soft margarine
6 oz (175 g) caster sugar
1 egg, beaten

10 oz (275 g) self-raising flour
4 oz (100 g) cornflakes, lightly
   crushed

Heat the oven to 375°F, 190°C, gas mark 5, and lightly grease two baking trays.

Measure the margarine and sugar into a bowl, and cream together until soft. Beat in the egg, then gradually work in the flour until the mixture has come together. Chill in the refrigerator for about 30 minutes.

Roll the mixture into small balls and then roll each one in the crushed cornflakes. Arrange, spaced well apart, on the trays and slightly flatten with the hand.

Bake in the oven for about 20–25 minutes, until turning pale golden brown at the edges.

Allow to cool for a few moments, then carefully lift off with a palette knife and finish cooling on a wire rack. Store in an airtight tin.

Makes about 34

MUESLI FLAPJACKS

A delicious variation on the flapjack theme. They're quick and easy to make.

4 oz (100 g) margarine   3 oz (75 g) rolled oats
4 oz (100 g) demerara sugar   2 oz (50 g) breakfast muesli
1 level tablespoon golden
  syrup

Heat the oven to 325°F, 160°C, gas mark 3, and lightly grease a 7 inch (18 cm) shallow square tin.

Measure the margarine into a pan with the sugar and syrup and heat gently until the margarine has melted. Remove from the heat and stir in the oats and muesli. Mix well then turn into the tin and level out evenly.

Bake in the oven for about 35 minutes until golden brown. Remove from the oven, leave to cool for 10 minutes then mark into 12 squares. Leave in the tin to finish cooling.

Makes 12

ICED GINGERBREAD SQUARES

Really moist and delicious, and icing them makes them very special.

5 oz (150 g) golden syrup
5 oz (150 g) black treacle
4 oz (100 g) light muscovado
   sugar
4 oz (100 g) soft margarine
8 oz (225 g) self-raising flour
1 teaspoon mixed spice

1 teaspoon ground ginger
2 eggs, lightly beaten
2 tablespoons milk

Topping
2 oz (50 g) crystallized ginger
8 oz (225 g) icing sugar

Grease and line with greased greaseproof paper a 12 × 8 inch (30 × 20 cm) oblong tin. Heat the oven to 325°F, 160°C, gas mark 3.

Measure the syrup, treacle, sugar and margarine into a pan and heat gently until the margarine has melted. Remove pan from the heat and stir in the flour and spices. Add the lightly beaten eggs and milk, and beat well until smooth. Pour into the prepared tin.

Bake in the oven for about 45 minutes, until well risen and the gingerbread is beginning to shrink slightly from the sides of the tin. Allow to cool in the tin for a few moments, then turn out and finish cooling on a wire rack.

Finely chop the ginger and sprinkle over the top of the cake. Sift the icing sugar into a bowl, add about 2 tablespoons water, and mix to a smooth paste. Put icing into a polythene bag, snip off one of the corners and drizzle random wiggly lines over the gingerbread. Leave to set.

Cuts into about 20 squares

SMALL LUXURY ROCK CAKES

Rock cakes are made so quickly from store-cupboard ingredients, and are full of fruit. I like mine to spread a bit as it makes them lighter. If you like a more solid rock cake, then just add 1 tablespoon milk. If you like spicy ones, add a level teaspoon of mixed spice.

8 oz (225 g) self-raising flour
2 teaspoons baking powder
4 oz (100 g) soft margarine
2 oz (50 g) golden granulated
   sugar
3 oz (75 g) sultanas

3 oz (75 g) currants
1 egg, beaten
2 tablespoons milk

Topping
a little demerara sugar

Heat the oven to 400°F, 200°C, gas mark 6, and lightly grease two large baking trays.

Measure the flour and baking powder into a bowl, add the margarine, and rub in until the mixture resembles breadcrumbs. Add the remaining ingredients and mix together. Spoon out 12 rock cakes on each baking tray using 2 teaspoons. Sprinkle each with demerara sugar.

Put the two trays one above the other in the oven, swapping the trays over half-way through the cooking time. Bake for about 15 minutes until just beginning to brown at the edges. Lift on to a wire rack to cool.

Makes 24 rock cakes

DROP SCONES

Quick and easy to make from ingredients likely already to be in the larder, and they're delicious warm spread with butter and strawberry jam.

4 oz (100 g) self-raising flour	1 egg
1 oz (25 g) caster sugar	¼ pint (150 ml) milk

Grease a heavy frying pan or griddle. Stand it on either the gas ring or electric plate on medium heat until hot.

Measure the flour and sugar into a bowl, make a well in the centre, add the egg and half the milk, and beat to a thick batter. Stir in the remaining milk.

Spoon the mixture on to the hot pan in tablespoonfuls, spacing them well apart. When bubbles rise to the surface, turn the pancakes over with a palette knife and cook on the other side for a further 30 seconds or so until golden brown.

Lift off and keep wrapped in a clean tea towel to keep them soft. Continue cooking until all the batter has been used, and then serve them warm.

Makes about 20 drop scones

AMERICAN ORANGE MEGA-MUFFINS

These delicious American muffins are served warm at breakfast, split and buttered, but of course are equally good at tea time.

10 oz (275 g) wholewheat self-raising flour
8 oz (225 g) white self-raising flour
4 oz (100 g) brown sugar
4 oz (100 g) sultanas
2 teaspoons baking powder
¼ pint (150 ml) milk
grated rind and juice of 2 oranges
1 egg
2 oz (50 g) butter, melted

Grease 9–12 large deep bun tins, and heat the oven to 375°F, 190°C, gas mark 5.

Measure both flours, sugar, sultanas and baking powder into a large bowl. Mix together in a separate bowl the milk, orange juice and rind, egg and melted butter. Pour into the dry ingredients and combine thoroughly, stirring with a fork. Spoon the mixture into the greased bun tins to come almost level with the top.

Bake in the oven for about 20–25 minutes, according to tin size, until the muffins are firm to the touch and a skewer pushed into them comes out clean. Leave them in the tins and cover with a clean tea towel until cool, when they will come out easily.

To serve, warm through, split, and spread with butter.

Makes 9–12 large muffins

ICE-BOX BISCUITS

Store these biscuits, uncut in the roll, in the fridge, and you will always have fresh baked biscuits in a matter of minutes.

4 oz (100 g) butter
8 oz (225 g) caster sugar
1 small egg, beaten

10 oz (225 g) plain flour
demerara sugar for rolling

Heat the oven to 375°F, 190°C, gas mark 5.

Cream together the butter and caster sugar, stir in the egg and work in the flour. When well mixed turn on to a flat surface and firm into a sausage shape. Roll the sausage in demerara sugar and wrap in foil. Place in the fridge to harden.

Cut slices from the roll with a sharp knife and place on a baking sheet. Bake in the oven for about 8 minutes until light golden. Cool on a wire rack.

Makes about 50 biscuits

MACAROONS

Delicious to serve as a very special biscuit with coffee after dinner.

2 egg whites
16 halved blanched almonds
4 oz (100 g) ground almonds

6 oz (175 g) caster sugar
1 oz (25 g) ground rice or
   semolina
a few drops of almond essence

Heat the oven to 300°F, 150°C, gas mark 2. Line two baking trays with non-stick silicone paper.

Put the egg whites into a bowl, dip the blanched almonds into them, then put to one side. Whisk the egg whites with an electric whisk until they form soft peaks. Gently fold in the ground almonds, sugar, ground rice and almond essence.

Spoon the mixture in teaspoonfuls on to the lined baking trays, and smooth out with the back of the spoon to form circles. Place one of the almonds in the centre of each.

Bake in the oven for about 25 minutes until a pale golden brown. Leave to cool on the trays for a few moments then lift off with a palette knife and finish cooling on a wire rack.

Makes about 16 macaroons

GLAZED STRAWBERRY TARTS

If liked, decorate the tarts with a swirl of whipped cream. Fill with other fruits as their seasons come round.

Tart Cases
4 oz (100 g) plain flour
2 oz (50 g) butter
1 tablespoon caster sugar
about 4 teaspoons water

Filling
12 oz (350 g) small fresh
  strawberries
3 tablespoons redcurrant jelly
1 tablespoon water

Heat the oven to 375°F, 190°C, gas mark 5.

Measure the sieved flour into a bowl. Cut the butter into small pieces, and rub into the flour until the mixture resembles fine breadcrumbs. Stir in the sugar and add sufficient water to make a firm dough. Ideally, wrap the pastry in clear film and chill for a while.

Roll out the pastry on a lightly floured surface and cut into rounds with a 2 inch (5 cm) fluted cutter. Use to line patty or bun tins, then chill in the refrigerator for about 15 minutes.

Line each case with a small piece of foil, then bake in the oven for about 10–15 minutes until pale golden brown. Remove the foil and allow to cool on a wire rack.

When the tartlet cases are cold, arrange the fresh strawberries in their centres. Heat the jelly and water in a small pan over a low heat until smooth. Spoon this glaze over the strawberries and leave to set.

Makes about 9 tarts

VERY SPECIAL CHEESE SCONES

Lovely to serve at a coffee morning, cheese scones make a nice alternative to all the sweet things usually on offer. However, it's easy to make more conventional scones – see the variation.

8 oz (225 g) self-raising flour
2 oz (50 g) butter
3 oz (75 g) well-flavoured
   Cheddar cheese, grated
¼ pint (150 ml) milk and
   water, mixed

To Serve
8 oz (225 g) cream cheese
2 tablespoons freshly snipped
   chives

Heat the oven to 425°F, 220°C, gas mark 7, and lightly grease a baking tray.

Measure the flour into a bowl. Cut the butter into small pieces, then rub into the flour until the mixture resembles fine breadcrumbs. Add the cheese and mix in enough of the milk and water to give a soft dough. Turn out on to a lightly floured surface and roll out thickly. With a plain cutter, cut into 1½ inch (4 cm) rounds.

Arrange on the tray, brush the tops with a little milk and bake in the oven for about 10–15 minutes until well risen and golden brown. Cool on a wire rack.

To serve, mix together the cream cheese and chives. Split open the scones and fill with some of the cream cheese.

Makes about 15 scones

Old-Fashioned Rich Tea Scones

Simply omit the cheese and stir 1 oz (25 g) sugar into the 'breadcrumb' mixture. You won't need so much milk and water.

LEMON CRUNCHY LOAVES

Quite one of my most favourite recipes. I have made it into a round cake and a traybake but this is the way we like it best, and it's so easy to slice. I've tried it with orange but it is nowhere near as good as lemon.

4 oz (100 g) soft margarine
6 oz (175 g) self-raising flour
1 level teaspoon baking
   powder
6 oz (175 g) caster sugar
2 eggs
4 tablespoons milk
finely grated rind of 1 lemon

Crunchy Icing
juice of 1 lemon
4 oz (100 g) caster or
   granulated sugar

Heat the oven to 350°F, 180°C, gas mark 4. Grease and line two 1 lb (450 g) loaf tins with greased greaseproof paper.

Measure the margarine, flour, baking powder, sugar, eggs, milk and lemon rind into a large bowl and beat well for about 2 minutes. Divide the mixture between the prepared tins, and level out evenly.

Bake for about 30 minutes, or until the cakes have shrunk slightly from the sides of the tins and spring back when lightly pressed with a finger.

Whilst the cakes are baking, measure the lemon juice and sugar into a bowl and stir until blended. When the loaves come out of the oven, spread the lemon paste over the top whilst the loaves are still hot. Leave in the tin until quite cold, then turn out, remove paper and store in an airtight tin.

Makes 2 loaves

W.I. MINCEMEAT FRUIT LOAVES

Many moons ago I invented the mincemeat cake and over the years I have varied the ingredients slightly. This version is made in 1 lb (450 g) loaf tins as on more than one occasion W.I. members have told me how useful it is to make and sell at W.I. markets. You can, of course, double up this recipe and bake four at a time; they're much easier to fit in the oven than round tins! But do remember that the more you fill the oven the longer anything will take to cook. (The exception is if you have a fan oven.)

2 eggs
5 oz (150 g) caster sugar
5 oz (150 g) soft margarine
8 oz (225 g) self-raising flour
12 oz (350 g) mincemeat
8 oz (225 g) currants

Topping
a few flaked almonds

Heat the oven to 325°F, 160°C, gas mark 3. Grease and line two 1 lb (450 g) loaf tins with greased greaseproof paper.

Crack the eggs into a large roomy bowl, then add all the other ingredients. Mix well until blended. Divide the mixture between the two tins and level out evenly. Sprinkle with flaked almonds.

Bake in the oven for about 1¼ hours until risen, pale golden brown and shrinking away from the sides of the tin. A fine skewer pushed into the centre of the loaves should come out clean.

Turn out of the tins and cool on a wire rack. Peel off paper and store in an airtight tin.

Makes 2 loaves

APPLE FRUIT TEABREAD

*All the teabread recipes I give freeze well, and because the
majority are made in loaf tins, they're easy to slice. Serve spread
with a little butter.*

4 oz (100 g) soft margarine
2 oz (50 g) golden granulated
　sugar
2 eggs
4 oz (100 g) mixed dried fruit
8 oz (225 g) self-raising
　wholewheat flour
1 large cooking apple, peeled,
　cored and chopped

2 tablespoons milk
1 teaspoon ground mixed
　spice

Topping
demerara sugar

Heat the oven to 350°F, 180°C, gas mark 4. Grease and line two
1 lb (450 g) loaf tins with greased greaseproof paper.

Measure all the ingredients into a bowl and mix well until
thoroughly blended. Divide equally between the tins and level
out evenly. Sprinkle with demerara sugar.

Bake in the oven for about 1 hour until risen. If cooked, a
skewer should come out clean when pushed into the centre of
the loaves.

Leave to cool in the tins for 2–3 minutes then turn out, peel off
paper and finish the cooling on a wire rack.

Makes 2 loaves

BANANA CHERRY LOAF

Served in thin slices, this loaf is perfect for a coffee morning.
Remember to wash and dry the cherries before using.

8 oz (225 g) self-raising flour
4 oz (100 g) soft margarine
6 oz (175 g) caster sugar

4 oz (100 g) glacé cherries,
   quartered
2 large bananas, mashed
2 eggs, beaten

Heat the oven to 350°F, 180°C, gas mark 4. Grease and line two
1 lb (450 g) loaf tins with greased greaseproof paper.

Measure all the ingredients into a bowl and mix well until
thoroughly blended. Divide the mixture between the two tins
and level out evenly.

Bake in the oven for about 1 hour until well risen. A skewer
should come out clean when pushed into the centre of the
loaves.

Leave to cool in the tins for 2–3 minutes, then turn out, peel off
paper and finish the cooling on a wire rack.

Makes 2 loaves

FRUIT TRAYBAKE

This is the sort of recipe which is quick and easy to prepare, and is perfect to cater for large family gatherings, coffee mornings and school fêtes.

6 oz (175 g) soft margarine
8 oz (225 g) self-raising flour
1½ level teaspoons baking
   powder
6 oz (175 g) caster sugar
3 eggs

3 tablespoons milk
8 oz (225 g) currants

Topping
2 level tablespoons demerara
   sugar

Heat the oven to 350°F, 180°C, gas mark 4. Grease and line a roasting tin about 12 × 9 inches (30 × 23 cm) with greased greaseproof paper.

Measure all the ingredients into a large bowl and beat well together until thoroughly blended. Turn into the tin and level the top out evenly.

Bake in the oven for about 20 minutes. Sprinkle the sugar evenly over the top of the cake and continue to cook for a further 15–20 minutes until the cake has shrunk slightly from the sides of the tin and is well risen.

Leave to cool in the tin. Cut into 21 pieces to serve.

Makes 21 pieces

DATE AND WALNUT CAKE

This cake keeps well, and is delicious served spread with a little butter. Why not use this, or one of the other teabreads, in sandwiches for a child's packed lunch – with a mashed banana and honey filling, for instance.

7 fl oz (210 ml) boiling water
6 oz (175 g) dates, chopped
¾ level teaspoon bicarbonate
  of soda
6 oz (175 g) light muscovado
  sugar

2 oz (50 g) soft margarine
1 egg, beaten
8 oz (225 g) self-raising flour
2 oz (50 g) walnuts, chopped

Heat the oven to 350°F, 180°C, gas mark 4. Grease and line an 8 inch (20 cm) square cake tin with greased greaseproof paper.

Measure the water, dates and bicarbonate of soda into a bowl and leave to stand for about 5 minutes.

Put the sugar and margarine into a bowl and cream together, then beat in the egg and the date mixture. Fold in the flour together with the walnuts and mix lightly until thoroughly blended. Turn the mixture into the tin and level out evenly.

Bake in the oven for about an hour until risen and slightly shrinking away from the sides of the tin. A skewer should come out clean when pushed into the centre of the cake.

Leave to cool in the tin for a few minutes, then turn out, peel off paper and finish cooling on a wire rack.

APRICOT FRUIT LOAF

This is such a good basic moist fruit cake, simple to slice and it doesn't crumble. There's no need to use first quality whole apricots, pieces will do fine. Wash and dry the cherries well.

2 large eggs
4 oz (100 g) self-raising flour
3 oz (75 g) soft margarine
3 oz (75 g) light muscovado
   sugar

2 oz (50 g) glacé cherries,
   quartered
3 oz (75 g) apricot pieces,
   chopped
3 oz (75 g) sultanas

Heat the oven to 325°F, 160°C, gas mark 3. Grease and line a 1 lb (450 g) loaf tin with greased greaseproof paper.

Break the eggs into a large bowl, add all the other ingredients, and beat well until smooth. Turn into the prepared tin and level the top.

Bake in the oven for about an hour until golden brown, firm to the touch and shrinking away from the sides of the tin. A fine skewer pushed into the centre of the cake should come out clean.

Leave to cool in the tin. Remove paper then store in an airtight tin.

SCRUMPY TEABREAD

A sound fruit loaf, which slices well without crumbling. It's best thinly sliced and buttered.

4 oz (100 g) currants
4 oz (100 g) raisins
4 oz (100 g) soft light brown
   sugar

⅓ pint (200 ml) sweet cider
1 egg, beaten
8 oz (225 g) self-raising flour

Soak the fruit and sugar in the cider overnight in an ovenglass bowl with a plate on top.

Grease and line a 2 lb (900 g) loaf tin with greased greaseproof paper. Heat the oven to 325°F, 160°C, gas mark 3.

Add the egg and flour to the fruit mixture and mix very well. Turn into the tin and level the top.

Bake in the oven for about 1–1¼ hours until golden brown and shrinking away from the sides of the tin.

Leave to cool in the tin, then remove paper and store in an airtight tin.

Cakes for the Children

The recipes here consist of some that the children can make themselves and some that they will merely enjoy eating! A few are suitable for making for birthday tea parties, and you can turn to the next chapter for some unusual birthday cake suggestions.

On wet days, or in the school holidays when not much is going on, children love to help in the kitchen. If they're quite young, allow plenty of time for this, and whatever age they are watch them carefully all the time as the kitchen is full of potential hazards in the form of sharp knives, heat, etc.

The party multi cakes and the gingerbread men are recipes which any child would enjoy helping with, as there's so much scope for individual creativity.

And don't expect any of these cakes to last too long – there's nothing quite like eating something you've made yourself!

PARTY MULTI CAKES

This basic mixture will make a variety of small buns which are perfect for small children who find a slice of cake a bit overpowering. Take care not to fill the cases too full so that there is room for the icing.

Basic Mixture
6 oz (175 g) soft margarine
6 oz (175 g) caster sugar
6 oz (175 g) self-raising flour
3 eggs
1½ level teaspoons baking
    powder

Additions (see method)
2 oz (50 g) chocolate polka
    dots
2 tablespoons cocoa, sieved
1 tablespoon milk
grated rind of 1 lemon

Lemon Butter Cream
2 oz (50 g) soft margarine
6 oz (175 g) icing sugar, sieved
1 tablespoon lemon juice

Toppings
a little extra icing sugar to
    dust
jelly beans
a little glacé icing (see
    page 16) made with 4 oz
    (100 g) sieved icing sugar
miniature chocolate flakes

Heat the oven to 400°F, 200°C, gas mark 6, and have ready about 30 paper cases set in bun tins.

For the basic mixture, measure the margarine, sugar, flour, eggs and baking powder into a bowl and beat well for 2–3 minutes until they are well blended and smooth.

Divide the mixture into three parts in separate bowls. Into one stir the polka dots, into another the cocoa and milk, and into the third the lemon rind. Divide the mixtures between the paper cases, filling about 10 cases with each flavour.

Bake in the oven for about 15 minutes until the cakes are well risen and spring back when lightly pressed with a finger. Lift out and cool on a wire rack.

For the butter cream, beat together the margarine and icing sugar with the lemon juice until smooth. Cut a slice from the top of each of the lemon-flavoured buns, and cut this slice in half. Spoon a blob of the butter cream into the centre and place the two half slices of cake into the icing, butterfly-wing fashion. Dust with a little icing sugar. (Alternatively, these lemon cakes could be topped with a glacé icing made with lemon juice, and then decorated with a jelly bean.)

To decorate the cocoa-flavoured cakes, spread a little of the glacé icing on top, and decorate with a miniature chocolate flake. The polka-dot cakes don't need any topping decoration.

Makes about 30 cakes

FUDGE-TOPPED ICE CREAM CAKE

Keep the leftover fudge sauce in a jar in the fridge to serve with this delicious cake. (It will keep for up to four weeks.)

1 × 8 inch (20 cm) bought   *Fudge Sauce*
   sponge flan case   2 oz (50 g) butter
1 litre carton vanilla ice cream   5 oz (150 g) golden granulated
                                     sugar
                              1 × 6 oz (175 g) can
                                 evaporated milk

To make the fudge sauce, measure all the ingredients into a saucepan, and heat gently until the sugar has dissolved completely. Bring to the boil for about 5 minutes until pale golden and still runny. Allow to cool until it is of a coating consistency.

Fill the sponge flan case with ice cream, smooth the top and cover with some of the fudge sauce. Put into the freezer until thoroughly chilled, then serve. To freeze, cover with clear film, put in a freezer bag and label. Thaw 15 minutes before serving.

Serves 8

CHOCOLATE MALLOW SLICES

A real favourite with children and easy enough for them to make themselves. They're quite sticky and messy to eat, so it's a good idea to supply forks and napkins! Remember to wash and dry the cherries well before chopping.

Base
4 oz (100 g) margarine
2 tablespoons cocoa, sieved
4 oz (100 g) icing sugar, sieved
1 egg
1 teaspoon vanilla essence
3½ oz (90g) desiccated
  coconut
6 oz (175 g) digestive biscuits,
  crushed

Topping
cold water
8 oz (225 g) caster sugar
2 teaspoons gelatine
2 oz (50 g) glacé cherries,
  finely chopped

For the base, measure the margarine, cocoa and icing sugar into a pan and heat gently until the margarine has melted. Add the remaining ingredients and mix thoroughly. Spread evenly into an 8 × 12 inch (20 × 30 cm) oblong tin and put in the fridge to set.

For the topping, measure 3 tablespoons water and the sugar into a bowl and whisk with an electric whisk for 5 minutes until the mixture becomes creamy. Mix the gelatine with 3 more tablespoons of water and leave until spongy; dissolve by standing the bowl over a pan of simmering water. Whisk this into the sugar mixture until stiff. Fold in the cherries and spread over the chocolate base. Return to the fridge until set. Serve in small slices.

Makes about 30 small slices

CHOCOLATE PASSION CAKES

*These are best stored in, and served straight from, the fridge.
Wash and dry the cherries before chopping.*

8 oz (225 g) milk chocolate,
     broken into small pieces
8 oz (225 g) block margarine
2 eggs
8 oz (225 g) Nice biscuits
2 oz (50 g) glacé cherries,
     chopped

2 oz (50 g) almonds, chopped

Decoration
¼ pint (150 ml) double cream,
     whipped
chocolate buttons

Measure the chocolate and margarine into a bowl over a pan of
simmering water and heat very gently until melted. Remove
from the heat and beat in the eggs until blended.

Roughly break up the biscuits, and stir into the chocolate
mixture with the cherries and almonds. Divide between 12
paper cases, level out and leave to set in the refrigerator
overnight until firm.

Serve decorated with a swirl of cream and chocolate buttons.

Makes 12 cakes

CHOCOLATE KRISPIES

My young enjoyed chocolate krispies from the year dot, and were soon able to make them themselves which they loved doing. I always make them small, putting them in sweet paper cases, and usually add a few sultanas. I use whichever cereal is left – cornflakes, wheatflakes or Rice Krispies.

2 oz (50 g) butter
1 level tablespoon cocoa, sieved
1 rounded tablespoon golden syrup

2½ oz (60 g) Rice Krispies
2 oz (50 g) sultanas

Melt the butter in a fairly large saucepan, then stir in the cocoa and golden syrup. Mix well and remove from the heat. Add Krispies and sultanas. Spoon into paper sweet cases and leave to set for 30 minutes (if you can!).

Makes about 20 krispies

KRISPIE CRUNCHY CAKES

Always popular with the young at birthday party teas. This is a very versatile recipe which can be altered according to what you happen to have in the store cupboard at the time.

6 oz (175 g) plain chocolate, broken into small pieces
5 oz (150 g) block margarine, cut in pieces
1 egg
1 oz (25 g) caster sugar
4 oz (100 g) digestive biscuits
2 oz (50 g) Rice Krispies
1 oz (25 g) walnuts, chopped
1 oz (25 g) almonds, chopped
2 oz (50 g) raisins, chopped
2 oz (50 g) glacé cherries, washed, dried and quartered

Measure the chocolate and margarine into a bowl and stand over a pan of simmering water to melt. Remove from the heat and stir in the egg and sugar.

Roughly break up the biscuits and stir into the mixture together with the Rice Krispies, walnuts, almonds, raisins and cherries. Divide between 15 paper cases and leave to set.

Makes about 15 cakes

CHOCOLATE CHIP COOKIES

These light crisp biscuits are so easy and quick to make, and children love shaping them (as well as eating them).

8 oz (225 g) soft margarine   10 oz (275 g) self-raising flour
6 oz (175 g) caster sugar   4 oz (100 g) chocolate chips
1 egg, beaten

Lightly grease some baking sheets, and heat the oven to 350°F, 180°C, gas mark 4.

Measure the margarine and sugar into a bowl and beat until creamy. Add the egg, flour and chocolate chips, and blend well together.

With wet hands form the mixture into balls about the size of large marbles and place spaced well apart on the greased baking sheets. Press lightly with a fork.

Bake in the oven for about 15 minutes until pale golden then cool on the sheets for a few minutes before moving to a wire rack.

Makes about 60 cookies

CHILLED CHOCOLATE AND RAISIN SQUARES

Very rich and special, so serve in quite small squares.

6 oz (175 g) plain chocolate,   2 oz (50 g) raisins
   broken into small pieces
4 oz (100 g) butter   *To Decorate*
1 × 6 oz (175 g) can condensed   chocolate raisins
   milk
10 oz (275 g) digestive biscuits

Line an 11 × 7 inch (28 × 18 cm) Swiss roll tin with silicone paper.

Measure the chocolate, butter and condensed milk into a pan and heat gently until melted, stirring occasionally. Roughly crumble the biscuits and stir into the mixture with the raisins. Mix well.

Turn the mixture into the lined tin and level out evenly. Arrange the chocolate raisins in clusters of three, so that when set and cut into squares, each square will have three chocolate raisins as decoration. Chill in the refrigerator until firm. Remove from tin, peel off paper and cut into squares.

Makes about 20 squares

SHARP LEMON SQUARES

These are like lemon sponge, and taste best filled with home-made lemon curd. Children in particular enjoy them as they are quite chewy.

4 eggs
finely grated rind of 1 lemon
4 oz (100 g) caster sugar, warmed
1 oz (25 g) cornflour
3 oz (75 g) self-raising flour

Filling
3 tablespoons lemon curd
a little lemon glacé icing

Grease and line a 13 × 9 inch (33 × 23 cm) Swiss roll tin with silicone paper. Heat the oven to 375°F, 190°C, gas mark 5.

Break the eggs into a large bowl, add the rind and sugar, and whisk with an electric whisk until the latter leaves a trail in the foamy mixture. Very carefully fold in the sieved flours a little at a time with a metal spoon. Tip into the prepared tin.

Bake in the oven for about 20 minutes until the sponge is shrinking away from the sides of the tin and is golden brown. Leave to cool in the tin for about 5 minutes. Peel off paper and finish cooling on a wire rack.

Cut in half (two rectangles of 9 × 6½ inches/23 × 16 cm). Spread one half generously with lemon curd and top with the second half. Dribble icing over the top. Cut into small squares.

Makes 16 squares

GINGERBREAD MEN

It is difficult to say just how many men this quantity of mixture will make as everyone has different sized cutters. The mixture doesn't spread on cooking so they can be cut out fairly close together. After the second rolling, form the leftover dough into a sausage shape and chill, then slice into discs and bake on a baking sheet for about 10 minutes.

2 oz (50 g) soft margarine
2 oz (50 g) caster sugar
4 oz (100 g) self-raising flour

½ teaspoon bicarbonate of
   soda
1 teaspoon ground ginger
about 1 tablespoon golden
   syrup

Heat the oven to 350°F, 180°C, gas mark 4. Lightly grease two large flat baking trays.

Measure the margarine into a bowl, add the sugar, and cream until light and creamy. Add the flour, bicarbonate of soda, ginger and syrup and work together to give a soft dough. Knead lightly.

Roll out the dough on one of the baking trays, and cut out with a gingerbread man cutter. Lift off the surplus dough, re-roll on to the other baking tray, and cut out. Bake in the oven for about 12–15 minutes until an even straw colour. Allow to cool on the tray for a few moments then lift on to a wire rack to finish cooling.

The gingerbread men can be decorated in a variety of ways:

1. Use chocolate polka dots for the eyes, nose, mouth and buttons and stick them on with a little lightly whisked egg white.

2. Make up a little icing and pipe on eyes, nose, mouth and buttons.

3. Pipe each child's name or initial on to a gingerbread man with a fine nozzle.

LEMON STARS

Children adore these crisp biscuits. If liked, for a special treat, dip in a little melted chocolate just to cover two points of the star.

8 oz (225 g) plain flour
4 oz (100 g) butter
4 oz (100 g) caster sugar
grated rind of 1 lemon

1 egg, lightly beaten

Decoration
a little icing sugar

Heat the oven to 350°F, 180°C, gas mark 4. Lightly grease two baking trays.

Measure the flour into a bowl and rub in the butter until the mixture resembles fine breadcrumbs. Stir in the sugar and lemon rind, and add just sufficient egg to give a firm dough. Wrap in clear film and chill in the refrigerator for about 20 minutes.

Roll out the dough on a lightly floured surface to about ¼ inch (6 mm) thick. With a star-shaped cutter, cut out the biscuits and arrange on the baking sheets, leaving room for them to spread a little.

Bake in the oven for about 12 minutes until a pale straw colour. Allow to cool slightly then lift off with a palette knife and finish cooling on a wire rack.

To decorate, dust with a little sieved icing sugar.

Makes about 32 biscuits, depending on the size of the cutter

PINWHEEL BISCUITS

Easy enough for children, giving an attractive contrast of colours.

4 oz (100 g) soft margarine	a few drops of vanilla essence
2 oz (50 g) caster sugar	1 level tablespoon cocoa
2 oz (50 g) cornflour	powder, sieved
4 oz (100 g) plain flour	milk

Heat the oven to 350°F, 180°C, gas mark 4 and grease two baking sheets.

Measure half the margarine and half the sugar into a bowl and cream together until pale and fluffy. Mix the cornflour and plain flour together. Gradually work in half the flour and the vanilla essence. Knead well, wrap in foil and put in the fridge to chill for about 30 minutes.

Meanwhile cream the rest of the margarine and sugar as before, then add the remaining flour and the cocoa powder. Knead and wrap, and chill in the fridge.

Roll out both pieces of dough to oblongs about 10 × 7 inches (25 × 18 cm). Brush a little milk on one layer and place the second piece on top. Roll up from the narrow edge and wrap in foil. Refrigerate for about 30 minutes.

Cut the roll into slices and place them on a baking sheet. Bake in the oven for about 10–15 minutes. Watch carefully: they are done when the pale part of the biscuit has just begun to turn a deep creamy colour.

Makes about 18 biscuits

Cakes for Special Occasions

Special occasions such as Christmas, weddings, christenings and major anniversaries require special cakes, and my celebration fruit cake recipe has been 'refined' to a high degree. Even if you've never attempted to make a rich fruit cake before, you'll find it easy as I've carefully worked out every possible permutation – the ingredient quantities, timings, all the extras such as almond paste and icings – for all sizes and shapes of cake tins.

Easter too requires its traditional fare. I like to make a Simnel cake, and some versions of the recipe have eleven almond paste balls around the top, rather than my sausage, to represent the eleven faithful disciples.

Birthdays are special occasions whether you're nine or ninety, and, using one or other of my two basic sponges, you can create a wealth of witty and entertaining cakes to suit the star of the day!

CELEBRATION CAKE

This recipe makes a shallow cake rather than the more usual deep cake. I find that when the cake has been almond pasted and iced you can get a slice that is really too big. So if you prefer a deeper fruit cake, step up one size of mixture on the chart using the smaller tin.

Kitchens are warmer than they used to be and few of us have cool larders. If you want to make this rich fruit cake three months ahead: cool, wrap in greaseproof proof or silicone paper, then wrap again in foil and store in the freezer.

Take care to line the cake tin well; it is so infuriating to be unable to get it out of the tin easily. Ovens do vary so if you notice that the top of the cake is getting too brown just slip a piece of foil loosely over the top.

3 months ahead: *Make the cake, cool, wrap in clear film and then with foil. Store in a cool place.*

4 weeks ahead: *Almond paste the cake.*

2 weeks ahead: *Royal or fondant ice the cake.*

1 week ahead: *Decorate the cake.*

Ingredient Quantities for Celebration Cake (Imperial)

Round tin	Square tin	Mixed dried fruit	Glacé cherries	Dried apricot pieces	Sherry	Soft marg
7″	6″	8 oz	4 oz	4 oz	2.5 fl. oz	4 oz
8″	7″	1 lb	8 oz	8 oz	¼ pt	6 oz
9″	8″	1½ lb	12 oz	12 oz	¼ pt	9 oz
10″	9″	2 lb	1 lb	1 lb	½ pt	12 oz
11″	10″	2½ lb	1¼ lb	1¼ lb	½ pt	15 oz
12″	11″	3 lb	1½ lb	1½ lb	¾ pt	1 lb 2 oz
13″	12″	3½ lb	1¾ lb	1¾ lb	¾ pt	1 lb 5 oz

Ingredient Quantities for Celebration Cake (Imperial) (*contd*)

Round tin	Dark brown sugar	Eggs	Chopped blanched almonds	Black treacle	Self-raising flour	Plain flour	Ground mixed spice
7"	4 oz	2	1 oz	½ tblsp	2 oz	2 oz	½ tsp
8"	6 oz	3	2 oz	1 tblsp	2 oz	4 oz	1 tsp
9"	9 oz	5	3 oz	1 tblsp	3 oz	6 oz	1½ tsp
10"	12 oz	6	4 oz	2 tblsp	4 oz	8 oz	2 tsp
11"	15 oz	7	5 oz	2 tblsp	5 oz	10 oz	2½ tsp
12"	1 lb 2 oz	9	6 oz	3 tblsp	6 oz	12 oz	3 tsp
13"	1 lb 5 oz	10	7 oz	3 tblsp	7 oz	14 oz	3½ tsp

Ingredient Quantities for Celebration Cake (Metric)

Round tin	Square tin	Mixed dried fruit	Glacé cherries	Dried apricot pieces	Sherry	Soft marg
18 cm	15 cm	225 g	100 g	100 g	75 ml	100 g
20 cm	18 cm	450 g	225 g	225 g	150 ml	175 g
23 cm	20 cm	675 g	350 g	350 g	150 ml	250 g
25 cm	23 cm	900 g	450 g	450 g	300 ml	350 g
28 cm	25 cm	1.25 kg	550 g	550 g	300 ml	425 g
30 cm	28 cm	1.5 kg	675 g	675 g	450 ml	500 g
33 cm	30 cm	1.5 kg	800 g	800 g	450 ml	575 g

Round tin	Dark brown sugar	Eggs	Blanched chopped almonds	Black treacle	Self-raising flour	Plain flour	Ground mixed spice
18 cm	100 g	2	25 g	½ tblsp	50 g	50 g	½ tsp
20 cm	175 g	3	50 g	1 tblsp	50 g	100 g	1 tsp
23 cm	250 g	5	75 g	1 tblsp	75 g	175 g	1½ tsp
25 cm	350 g	6	100 g	2 tblsp	100 g	225 g	2 tsp
28 cm	425 g	7	150 g	2 tblsp	150 g	275 g	2½ tsp
30 cm	500 g	9	175 g	3 tblsp	175 g	350 g	3 tsp
33 cm	575 g	10	200 g	3 tblsp	200 g	400 g	3½ tsp

Baking Times for Celebration Cake

Round tin	Square tin	Total baking time about	at 300°F, 150°C, gas mark 2	at 275°F, 140°C, gas mark 1
7 inch (18 cm)	6 inch (15 cm)	2¾ hrs	2 hrs	¾ hrs
8 inch (20 cm)	7 inch (18 cm)	3¼ hrs	2 hrs	1¼ hrs
9 inch (23 cm)	8 inch (20 cm)	3½ hrs	2 hrs	1½ hrs
10 inch (25 cm)	9 inch (23 cm)	3¾ hrs	2 hrs	1¾ hrs
11 inch (28 cm)	10 inch (25 cm)	4¼ hrs	2 hrs	2¼ hrs
12 inch (30 cm)	11 inch (28 cm)	4¾ hrs	2 hrs	2¾ hrs
13 inch (33 cm)	12 inch (30 cm)	5 hrs	2 hrs	3 hrs

METHOD FOR CELEBRATION CAKE

First prepare the fruit. Quarter the washed and dried cherries and snip the apricot pieces. Put the mixed dried fruit, cherries and apricots into a container and pour the sherry over it. Cover with a lid and leave to soak for at least three days, stirring daily.

Heat the oven to the higher temperature, and grease and line the appropriate-sized tin with greased greaseproof paper.

Put the margarine, sugar, eggs, almonds and treacle into a large bowl. Sift together the flours and spice and add to the bowl. Mix together until evenly blended. Stir in the soaked fruit and sherry.

Turn the mixture into the prepared tin and level the top. Bake in the oven for the time suggested on the chart above, lowering the oven temperature as and when indicated. If making several tiers for a cake, the best results are obtained by baking one tier at a time. To check when the cake is done, pierce through the centre of the cake with a warm skewer; if it comes out clean, then the cake is cooked. If not, cook for a further 15 minutes. If during the cooking time the cake seems to be getting too brown on top, cover it very loosely with a sheet of foil.

Leave to cool completely in the tin.

ALMOND PASTE

I actually prefer now to buy ready prepared almond paste. There are some excellent makes available and it tends to work out cheaper than buying the ingredients and preparing it yourself. However, here is the basic recipe in case you do want to make your own.

8 oz (225 g) ground almonds	4 egg yolks, or 2 whole size 3
8 oz (225 g) caster sugar	eggs
8 oz (225 g) icing sugar, sieved	about 6 drops almond essence

Mix the ground almonds and sugars together in a bowl, then add the yolks or whole eggs and almond essence. Knead together to form a stiff paste. Do not over-knead as this will make the paste oily.

Store wrapped in clear film in the refrigerator until required.

Makes about 1½ lb (675 g)

TO COVER A CAKE WITH ALMOND PASTE

Stand the cake on a cake board, and brush the cake all over with a little apricot glaze.

Lightly dust a work surface with sieved icing sugar then roll out the paste to about 2 inches (5 cm) larger than the surface of the cake. Carefully lift the paste over the cake with the help of a rolling pin. Level and smooth out with your hand, then smooth the sides. Trim off at the base.

Alternatively, you may find it easier to cut a separate circle of almond paste for the top and strips for the sides of the cake. Stick these on to the cake with a little apricot glaze.

Quantities of Almond Paste

To cover both the sides and top of the cake.

Round tin	Square tin	Almond paste
7 inch (18 cm)	6 inch (15 cm)	1 lb (450 g)
8 inch (20 cm)	7 inch (18 cm)	1½ lb (675 g)
9 inch (23 cm)	8 inch (20 cm)	1¾ lb (800 g)
10 inch (25 cm)	9 inch (23 cm)	2 lb (900 g)
11 inch (28 cm)	10 inch (25 cm)	2¼ lb (1 kg)
12 inch (30 cm)	11 inch (28 cm)	2½ lb (1.1 kg)
13 inch (33 cm)	12 inch (30 cm)	3 lb (1.3 kg)

HOME-MADE FONDANT ICING

There are some excellent makes of fondant icing available on the market today. However, if you would prefer to prepare your own, then here is the recipe. Liquid glucose may be bought from good chemists, and is quite reasonably priced.

about 1 lb 2 oz (500 g) icing
   sugar

1 generous tablespoon liquid
   glucose
1 egg white

Sieve the icing sugar into a large mixing bowl, make a well in the centre and add the liquid glucose and egg white. Knead together until the mixture forms a soft ball.

Turn on to a surface sprinkled with sieved icing sugar, and knead for about 10 minutes until brilliant white. Keep adding sieved icing sugar if the mixture is a bit on the sticky side. Any colouring may be added at this stage.

Store in the refrigerator wrapped in clear film until required.

Makes about 1¼ lb (550 g)

To cover a cake with fondant icing

Brush the almond-pasted cake with sherry, rum or Kirsch (this has a sterilizing effect).

Roll out the icing to 2 inches (5 cm) larger than the cake on a table sprinkled with sieved icing sugar. Lift the icing on to the cake using the rolling pin for support. Smooth out evenly over the cake with your hand, and trim off at the base. Prick any air bubbles sideways with a pin, then finish smoothing with a plastic smoother or, carefully, with your hand.

Ideally, leave for seven days to dry out before decorating.

Quantities of Fondant Icing

To cover both the sides and top of the cake.

Round tin	Square tin	Fondant icing
8 inch	7 inch	1½ lb (675 g)
(20 cm)	(18 cm)	
9 inch	8 inch	1¾ lb (800 g)
(23 cm)	(20 cm)	
10 inch	9 inch	2¼ lb (1 kg)
(25 cm)	(23 cm)	
11 inch	10 inch	2¾ lb (1.2 kg)
(28 cm)	(25 cm)	
12 inch	11 inch	3 lb (1.3 kg)
(30 cm)	(28 cm)	

ROYAL ICING

I no longer flat ice a celebration cake with royal icing as I find I achieve a far superior result by using fondant icing but use royal icing for piping and decorating the cake. This quantity is sufficient to decorate a three-tier wedding cake. For a single layer cake prepare half this quantity.

To keep from drying out once made, cover with a damp J-cloth or damp muslin cloth, then cover with foil and keep in a cool place.

2 egg whites
1 lb 2 oz (500 g) icing sugar,
    sieved

about 4 teaspoons lemon juice

Put the egg whites into a large mixing bowl and whisk lightly with a fork until bubbles begin to form on the surface. Add about half the icing sugar and the lemon juice, and beat well with a wooden spoon for about 10 minutes until brilliant white. Gradually stir in the remaining icing sugar until the correct consistency for piping.

SIMPLE ROYAL ICED CHRISTMAS CAKE

These quantities are for an 8 inch (20 cm) round, almond paste covered cake (see page 123).

2 × royal icing recipe (see page 125)
10 inch (25 cm) round silver cake board
3–4 oz (75–100 g) almond paste
red, green and blue food colourings

1 red candle
ribbon to decorate
sugar bells (see page 127)

Put a little of the royal icing on to the silver cake board and stand the cake on top. The icing will secure the cake to the board. Put one-third of the icing into a small bowl and cover with clear film. Try drawing the remaining icing up into peaks; if it is too stiff, add a few drops of water to soften it. Put a tablespoon of icing aside, covered, to use later for securing the decorations. Spread the icing thickly round the sides of the cake, a few inches at a time. With a palette knife draw icing into peaks as you go. Put the cake on one side for an hour or two to let the icing harden.

Add just enough water to the icing in the small bowl to make it the consistency of thick glacé icing. Have ready a pin. Pour the thinned icing over the top of the cake spreading it just to the edges. Prick any air bubbles with the pin as they rise to the surface. Leave overnight for the icing to set.

Take about a quarter of the almond paste and colour this red. Roll the paste into small balls the size of the holly berries and set them on one side to dry.

Colour the remaining almond paste, using green and a very little blue to make the paste dark green. Roll the paste out on a board that has been lightly sprinkled with icing sugar. Using a ruler as a guide, cut the paste into 1 inch (2.5 cm) wide strips and cut these into diamonds. With the base of an icing nozzle remove small half circles from the sides of the diamonds, to give you holly-shaped leaves. Make vein marks on the leaves with a sharp knife. Bend the leaves over handles of wooden spoons to dry.

When the icing on the cake has set hard, put the candle on top of the cake, securing it with royal icing. Arrange sugar bells, ribbon and, if you like, holly leaves and berries around the candle.

SUGAR BELLS

To make sugar bells you will need to buy a hollow plastic or metal Christmas bell decoration to serve as a mould. Remove the clapper.

2 oz (50 g) caster sugar	white royal or glacé icing
egg white	silver balls (made of foil)

Place the sugar in a bowl and add just enough egg white to moisten the sugar, until it looks like damp sand. Spoon the mixture into the bell mould, pushing it well down, then turn it out. Tap the rim of the bell until the sugar shape comes out. Leave the bell until the outside is dry enough to handle but the centre is still moist. Carefully scoop out the centre with a knife point or cocktail stick. Pipe a little icing into the bell and top with a silver ball (made out of a little foil) for a clapper.

CHOCOLATE YULE LOG

For the Swiss roll use the recipe for Chocolate Swiss Roll on page 68, and roll up as suggested with the greaseproof paper in the middle. Leave to cool and then assemble as below.

1 unfilled chocolate Swiss roll
(see page 68)

12 oz (350 g) icing sugar, sieved

Butter Cream
2 tablespoons cocoa, sieved
3 tablespoons boiling water
6 oz (175 g) soft margarine

Decoration
a little icing sugar
a robin ornament and holly
leaves

For the butter cream, measure the cocoa into a bowl, add the water then mix to a smooth paste. Add the margarine and sugar and beat well until smooth and blended.

Unroll the Swiss roll, remove the paper, and carefully spread one-third of the butter cream on to the sponge, then re-roll.

Cut a small piece off at an angle from one of the ends of the Swiss roll. Place the long piece on a board and stick the smaller piece on to the side so that it looks like a branch.

Put the remaining butter cream into a piping bag fitted with a small star nozzle. Pipe long lengths of butter cream all along the length of the log to cover it completely. Pipe swirls of butter cream on to each of the ends.

Dust with a little icing sugar and decorate with the robin and holly leaves.

EASTER SIMNEL CAKE

This is now the traditional Easter cake, but originally it was given by servant girls to their mothers on Mothering Sunday.

6 oz (175 g) soft margarine or butter
6 oz (175 g) light soft brown sugar
3 eggs
6 oz (175 g) self-raising flour
2 level teaspoons mixed spice
10 oz (275 g) mixed dried fruit
2 oz (50 g) ground almonds

1 lb (450 g) almond paste (see page 122)

Decoration
a little pale yellow glacé icing made with 6 oz (175 g) icing sugar
sugar eggs and chickens

Heat the oven to 325°F, 160°C, gas mark 3. Grease and line an 8 inch (20 cm) round cake tin with greased greaseproof paper.

Put all the cake ingredients, except for the almond paste, into a large mixing bowl and beat well with a wooden spoon until well blended. Place half the mixture in the bottom of the tin and level out the top.

Take 12 oz (350 g) of the almond paste and roll out to a circle the size of the tin and then place on top of the cake mixture. Cover with the remaining cake mixture and level the top.

Bake in the oven for about 1½ hours until evenly browned and shrinking away slightly from the sides of the tin. Leave in the tin to cool for about 10 minutes, then turn out, peel off the paper and finish cooling on a wire rack.

With the remaining almond paste, make a long sausage then lay this in a circle round the outside top of the cake. Pour the icing into the centre of the circle and leave to set. Decorate with sugar eggs and chickens.

BIRTHDAY CAKE GENOESE SPONGE

The sponge is moist and light so you can make it one day and ice and decorate it the next. Use this recipe or the Victoria Sponge opposite as a base for the party cakes which follow.

5 oz (150 g) self-raising flour	6 oz (175 g) caster sugar
1 oz (25 g) cornflour	2 tablespoons sunflower oil
6 eggs	

You will need the size of tin specified for the cake you are making, and the oven must be heated to the temperature given for that cake (see following recipes).

Sieve together the flour and cornflour. Put the eggs and sugar into a large bowl and whisk with an electric whisk until thick and pale in colour and the whisk leaves a trail when lifted out. Gently fold in the flours, then fold in the oil.

Turn into the prepared tin and bake in the oven for the time given for your particular cake, or until it is well risen and the centre of the sponge springs back when lightly pressed with a fingertip.

Cool as in the individual recipes.

BIRTHDAY CAKE VICTORIA SPONGE

If you haven't got an electric whisk, you may find it easier to make this, rather than the Genoese sponge opposite, as a base for the other birthday cakes.

8 oz (225 g) soft margarine
8 oz (225 g) caster sugar
4 eggs

8 oz (225 g) self-raising flour
2 level teaspoons baking powder

You will need the size of tin specified for the cake you are making, and the oven must be heated to the temperature given for that cake (see following recipes).

Measure all the ingredients into a large bowl and beat well for about 2 minutes until blended and smooth.

Turn into the prepared tin and bake in the oven for the time given for your particular cake, or until it is well risen and the centre of the sponge springs back when lightly pressed with a fingertip.

Cool as in the individual recipes.

SNOOKER TABLE

This is a great favourite with the boys.

Sponge
use basic recipe (see page 131)

Filling
strawberry jam

Topping and Decoration
4 oz (100 g) butter, softened
8 oz (225 g) icing sugar, sieved

1¼ lb (550 g) fondant icing
(see page 124), coloured
green

½ recipe royal icing (see page
125) half coloured brown
coloured round sweets for
snooker balls
thin wooden satay sticks for
cues

Heat the oven to 350°F, 180°C, gas mark 4, then grease and
line a roasting tin about 12 × 9 inches (30 × 23 cm) with
greased greaseproof paper.

Make up the sponge recipe as given, turn into the prepared tin
and bake in the oven for about 40 minutes, until the cake has
shrunk from the sides and the top springs back when lightly
pressed with a finger. Leave to cool in the tin then turn out and
peel off the paper.

Divide the cake in three layers horizontally, and sandwich
together with jam. Mix the butter and icing sugar together
until thoroughly blended and spread over the cake. Roll out the
fondant icing and use to cover the cake.

Pipe bold lines of the brown royal icing around the sides of the
cake to form the outside of the table. Pipe the markings on the
table in white icing with a fine nozzle. Use a little icing to
secure the balls on the table and lay the cues on the cake. Pipe
lattice 'pockets' on the sides of the cakes with the fine nozzle.

TREASURE TROVE CAKE

A pretty cake which is a winner with the girls.

Sponge
use basic recipe (see page 131)

Filling
4 good tablespoons lemon curd

Topping
2 tablespoons lemon curd
12 oz (350 g) almond paste
   (see page 122)

Icing
1 lb (450 g) fondant icing (see
   page 124)

Decoration
12 inch (30 cm) round silver
   cake board
gold braid
red and gold striped ribbon
1 large bag chocolate coins
   covered in gold foil

Heat the oven to 350°F, 180°C, gas mark 4. Grease and line a
9 inch (23 cm) deep round cake tin with greased greaseproof
paper.

Make up the sponge recipe as given, turn into the tin and level
out evenly. Bake in the oven for about 45 minutes, or until well
risen and the centre of the cake springs back when lightly
pressed with a finger. Leave to cool in the tin for a few moments
then lift out, peel off paper and finish cooling on a wire rack.

Divide the sponge into three horizontal layers using a sharp
knife, then sandwich back together with the lemon curd.
Spread the top and the sides of the cake with more lemon curd.
Roll out the almond paste and use to cover the cake thinly.
Allow to dry for about 4 hours then top with the fondant icing.

To decorate, stand the cake on the silver board and decorate
with the braid, ribbon and coins. Cut the braid into four lengths
and secure across the cake to give eight divisions of cake. Make
a big loopy bow with the red and gold ribbon and secure in the
middle of the cake. Stick the coins around the side of the cake,
securing them with a little icing.

HEART-SHAPED CAKE

This is a really pretty cake to make for a girl. If you don't want to use crystallized flowers, then use silk or fresh flowers instead.

Sponge
use basic recipe (see page 131)
grated rind of 2 lemons

Filling
strawberry jam or lemon curd

Topping
4 oz (100 g) butter, softened
8 oz (225 g) icing sugar, sieved

1 lb (450 g) fondant icing (see page 124), coloured pale green

Decoration
lace to go round bottom of cake
crystallized flowers

Heat the oven to 350°F, 180°C, gas mark 4, then grease and line a 9 inch (23 cm) heart-shaped tin with greased greaseproof paper (see page 13).

Make up the sponge recipe as given, and add the grated lemon rind to the mixture. Turn into the prepared tin and bake in the oven for 45–50 minutes until risen and the top springs back when lightly pressed with a finger. Leave to cool in the tin then turn out and peel off the paper.

Divide the cake into three layers horizontally, and sandwich back together with jam or lemon curd. Mix the butter and icing sugar together until thoroughly blended and spread over the cake. Roll out the fondant icing and use to cover the cake.

Decorate with lace and crystallized flowers. For a more personal note you could pipe on a birthday message.

To crystallize flowers
Beat a little egg white and brush this over flowers and leaves. Dust with caster sugar on both sides, then stand on a wire cake rack in a warm place until crisp and dry. This takes a few hours.

CASTLE CAKE

This always goes down well with the boys – particularly if they all have a soldier to take home after the party!

Sponge
use basic recipe (see page 131)

Butter Cream
2 oz (50 g) cocoa, sieved
3 tablespoons boiling water
4 oz (100 g) soft margarine
12 oz (350 g) icing sugar,
   sieved

Decoration
12 oz (350 g) almond paste
   (see page 122)
½ teaspoon cocoa
1 packet chocolate buttons
1 small paper flag
toy soldiers

Heat the oven to 350°F, 180°C, gas mark 4, and grease and line an 8 inch (20 cm) square cake tin with greased greaseproof paper.

Make up the sponge recipe as given, turn into the prepared tin and bake for about 45 minutes until well risen and springs back when lightly pressed with a finger. Leave to cool in the tin for a few minutes, then turn out, peel off paper and finish cooling on a wire rack.

For the butter cream, measure the cocoa into a bowl and mix to a smooth paste with the water. Allow to cool, then mix in the margarine and sugar until thoroughly blended.

For the 'brickwork', roll out the almond paste as thinly as possible on a lightly icing-sugared surface, then cut from this the different pieces, as follows:

2 strips = 6½ × 3 inches (16 × 8 cm)
1 strip = 8 × 3 inches (20 × 8 cm)
1 strip = 11 × 3 inches (28 × 8 cm)
1 rectangle = 8 × 6 inches (20 × 14 cm)

Along one long edge of each of the four strips, make cuts ½ inch (1 cm) deep, at ¾ inch (2 cm) intervals, then cut out alternate pieces to form the battlements. Repeat this along one long edge of the rectangle. Make 'brick' markings with the back of a knife on each piece of almond paste. Put pieces to one side.

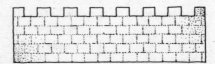

Roll the remaining scraps of almond paste into a small ball, flatten slightly and then work in the cocoa to make the paste dark brown. Roll out thinly to about a 2 inch (5 cm) square and cut into the shape of a double door by rounding off the two top corners. Put this on one side.

To assemble the cake, cut the sponge into three horizontal layers, then sandwich it together again with some of the butter cream. Cut a 1½ inch (4 cm) slice from one end of the sponge to make the fort which goes on top. Spread butter cream over the top of the large piece of sponge, then place the sponge slice for the fort on top, so that the cut edges of both pieces face towards the back and are aligned. Spread the remaining butter cream over all the surfaces of the sponge.

Lift the sponge on to a cake board before putting on the almond paste brickwork. Press the 11 × 3 inch (28 × 8 cm) strip around the sides and front of the sponge rectangle on top, and fix the 'door' on the front of this, using a little scraping of butter cream.

Press the 8 × 6 inch (20 × 14 cm) rectangle on to the back of the cake and to the fort. Place the 6½ × 3 inch (16 × 8 cm) strips of almond paste on each side of the cake. Arrange chocolate buttons in the 'courtyard' and also on the flat top of the fort to form paving stones. Lastly, place the 8 × 3 inch

(20 × 8cm) strip at the front. Press all the strips firmly on to the cake.

Put the flag and soldiers on top of the cake.

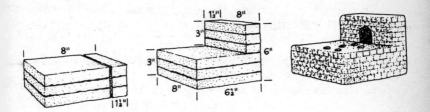

CATERPILLAR CAKE

This cake could equally well be made into a centipede or snake, depending on what sort of thing interests your child. Have ready a board made from a piece of thin card and covered with foil.

Sponge
use basic recipe on page 131, substituting 1 oz (25 g) cocoa powder for the cornflour

Butter Cream
3 oz (75 g) butter
6 oz (175 g) icing sugar, sieved
2 tablespoons milk
a few drops of peppermint essence

Decoration
1½ lb (675 g) fondant icing (see page 124)
a few drops of green food colouring
2 tablespoons apricot jam, sieved
1 tablespoon water
Liquorice Allsorts

Heat the oven to 375°F, 190°C, gas mark 5. Grease and line two 12 × 8 inch (30 × 20 cm) Swiss roll tins with greased greaseproof paper.

Make up the sponge recipe as given, divide between the two tins and bake in the oven for about 15 minutes, or until the sponges spring back when lightly pressed with a finger.

Whilst the sponges are cooking, cut two pieces of greaseproof paper slightly bigger than the tins, spread out on a work surface, and dust with caster sugar.

When the cakes come out of the oven invert them on to the sugared paper. Peel off the greaseproof paper from the bottom of the sponges, and trim all the edges. Make a score mark on each of the sponges, about ½ inch (1 cm) in from the edge and roll up each of the Swiss rolls with a clean sheet of greaseproof paper in the middle, using the score mark to start the rolling, and using the paper underneath to make a firm and even roll. Stand on wire racks and leave to cool completely.

For the butter cream, measure all the ingredients into a bowl and beat well until thoroughly blended.

When the Swiss rolls are cold, carefully unroll, remove the paper, spread each with butter cream, then roll up again. Trim a small piece at an angle from one end of a Swiss roll, then twist it slightly sideways, and use it as a wedge between the two Swiss rolls, so that the caterpillar's body curves a little in the middle. About 2 inches (5 cm) from the end scoop out a ring of cake to form a 'neck'.

Colour most of the fondant icing green and roll it out to a rectangle large enough to cover the Swiss rolls completely.

Arrange the Swiss rolls on the foil-covered board. Mix together the apricot jam and water and brush all over the caterpillar's body. Lift the fondant icing over the top of the Swiss rolls then tuck it in firmly underneath at each end. Squeeze in to form the neck. Colour a little fondant icing red and make into small circles, or spots, and stick these on the caterpillar with a little of the apricot mixture. Use the Liquorice Allsorts to make eyes, mouth and a tail.

GOLF BAG CAKE

This is the sort of novelty cake which is perfect for golf enthusiasts.

Make the icing the same colour as the bag the person actually uses for a more personal feel.

Sponge
use basic recipe (see page 131)

Filling
strawberry jam

Topping and Decoration
4 oz (100 g) butter, softened

8 oz (225 g) icing sugar, sieved
1¼ lb (600 g) fondant icing (see page 124)
food colouring of choice
a little royal icing (see page 125)
silver food colouring

Heat the oven to 350°F, 180°C, gas mark 4, then grease and line a roasting tin about 12 × 9 inches (30 × 23 cm) with greased greaseproof paper.

Make up the sponge recipe as given, turn into the prepared tin and bake in the oven for about 40 minutes, until the cake has shrunk from the sides and the top springs back when lightly pressed with a finger. Leave to cool in the tin then turn out and peel off the paper.

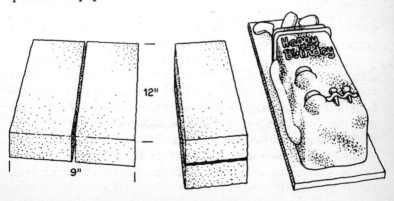

Divide the cake in half lengthwise to give two oblongs then sandwich one on top of the other with jam to give the base for the golf bag. Mix the butter and icing sugar together until thoroughly blended and spread all over the cake. Colour two-thirds of the fondant icing as you want, then roll out and use to cover the cake. With the remaining fondant icing, mould a handle for the bag, some tees and clubs. Stand the cake on a board and put the clubs in place. Stick the tees on to the bag with a little royal icing and pipe a birthday message on it too. Paint the tops of the clubs with edible silver food colouring to make them look authentic.

DARTBOARD CAKE

If you have got a dartboard at home, use this to copy the sequence of numbers so that the cake is really accurate!

Sponge
use basic recipe (page 131)

Filling
strawberry jam

Topping and Decoration
4 oz (100 g) butter, softened
8 oz (225 g) icing sugar, sieved
1 lb (450 g) fondant icing (see page 124)
red, yellow and black food colourings
a little royal icing (see page 125)

Heat the oven to 350°F, 180°C, gas mark 4 then grease and line a 9 inch (23 cm) deep round cake tin with greased greaseproof paper.

Make the sponge recipe as given and turn into the prepared tin. Bake in the oven for about 40–45 minutes until well risen and the top springs back when lightly pressed with a finger. Leave to cool in the tin, then turn out and peel off the paper.

Divide the cake in three layers horizontally and sandwich back together with jam. Mix the butter and icing sugar together until thoroughly blended and spread all over the cake. Roll out the fondant icing and completely cover the cake with it. Leave overnight to dry out.

Using a real dartboard as a guide, lightly mark out all the divisions on top of the cake. Paint in the appropriate colours using a fine paintbrush and food colouring. To finish the cake, pipe where the wires would be on a dartboard on to the top of the cake with the royal icing and a fine nozzle. Do the numbers too.

Continental Pastries and Cakes

On the Continent, there is a long and famous tradition of rich cakes and pastries. Each country seems to have its own particular speciality, some of which I've selected for this section. Many of the recipes here are longer and more complicated than elsewhere in the book, but they are all worthwhile and would make a spectacular centrepiece for a special tea or as a finale for a dinner party.

There is a cinnamon cake from Denmark – Scandinavian cakes and buns are often unusually spiced – and a recipe for Danish pastries which is quite different from the flabby offerings in so many cafés. There is a Swiss carrot cake, and a recipe for glazed tartlets from France. Also from France comes the multi-layered puff pastry confection, *millefeuilles*, and *vacherin*, a meringue topped with a mountain of chestnut purée (rather similar in conception to the Italian *monte bianco*). Rum babas, although they sound more eastern in promise, were first made for a king of Lorraine who, an enthusiastic reader of the *Thousand and One Nights*, named the new delight after one of its heroes, Ali Baba. From Germany and Austria come apple strüdels (made with bought Greek filo pastry), Viennese tea cakes, Doboz torte and Griestorte.

DANISH CINNAMON LAYER SHORTCAKE

This is also nice with a cherry filling, as a change from apple. Assemble just before serving, otherwise the shortcake will go soft.

6 oz (175 g) butter, softened
6 oz (175 g) caster sugar
8 oz (225 g) plain flour
2 level teaspoons ground
   cinnamon

Filling and Decoration
2 large Bramley apples,
   peeled, cored and sliced

1 teaspoon ground cinnamon
2 oz (50 g) demerara sugar
2 oz (50 g) butter
2 oz (50 g) sultanas
grated rind of 1 lemon
½ pint (300 ml) whipping
   cream, whipped
icing sugar, sieved
8 walnut halves

Heat the oven to 400°F, 200°C, gas mark 6, and lightly grease two large baking trays.

Cream the butter and sugar together in a bowl until light and fluffy. Add the flour and cinnamon a tablespoon at a time. The last few spoonfuls are easiest worked in by hand. Divide the mixture into four equal-sized pieces. Put one of the pieces on to a baking tray and press it out thinly with the fingers to form a circle about 8 inches (20 cm) in diameter. Repeat with the remaining pieces of dough.

Bake in the oven for about 12–15 minutes until just beginning to tinge with colour at the edges. Leave to cool for a few moments, then lift off carefully and finish cooling on a wire rack.

For the filling, gently cook the apples, cinnamon, demerara, butter, sultanas and lemon rind in a small pan until the apple is just tender. Allow to cool.

Sandwich the layers with the apple mixture and cream, leaving a little cream over for decoration. Dredge the top with icing sugar, then mark it into eight portions with a knife. Decorate each portion with a swirl of cream topped with a walnut half.

Serves 8

APPLE STRÜDELS

Wafer-thin pastry is characteristic of the Middle East and the Balkan area in general – think of the Arab pastries, the Greek baklavas *and, indeed, the Austrian* strüdels. *You can use Greek* filo *pastry for these strüdels, and you can of course make one big strüdel if preferred.*

3 sheets thicker strüdel
   pastry leaves
about 4 oz (100 g) butter,
   melted

1 oz (25 g) fresh brown
   breadcrumbs
2 oz (50 g) sultanas
1 level teaspoon ground
   cinnamon

Filling
1 lb (450 g) cooking apples,
   peeled, cored and roughly
   chopped
juice of ½ lemon
3 oz (75 g) demerara sugar

Topping
2 tablespoons caster sugar
2 tablespoons water
a little icing sugar, to dredge

For the filling, lightly mix together the apple, lemon juice, sugar, breadcrumbs, sultanas and cinnamon in a bowl.

Unfold one of the sheets of pastry and brush liberally with melted butter, then divide into four. Spoon one-sixth of the apple mixture along the shortest edge of one of the pieces of pastry, leaving a small border. Fold up this border, then roll the strüdel over and over, so the apple is secured in the centre. Lift this parcel on to another piece of the pastry and repeat the wrapping process. Lift on to the baking sheet. Repeat five more times until all the apple and pastry have been used. Brush each strüdel with more melted butter.

Cook in the oven for about 12–15 minutes until crisp and golden brown. Meanwhile blend the caster sugar and water together in a small pan and heat gently until all the sugar has dissolved. When the strüdels come out of the oven, carefully lift on to a serving plate. Spoon over the sugar syrup and dredge with a little icing sugar to serve.

Serves 6

DOBOZ TORTE

An extravagant speciality from Austria. Don't attempt to make this unless you really enjoy spending half the morning in the kitchen! It is a labour, but the result is stunning – six thin layers of sponge sandwich with rich butter cream, topped with caramel.

An electric whisk and a processor are a must for this recipe. The cooking time will depend on how many discs of sponge you cook at once and on the thickness of the baking trays.

Sponge
4 eggs
6 oz (175 g) caster sugar,
   warmed
5 oz (150 g) self-raising flour

Caramel
5 tablespoons water
6 oz (175 g) granulated or
   caster sugar

Butter Cream
1 heaped tablespoon cocoa
2 tablespoons boiling water
10 oz (275 g) icing sugar
6 oz (175 g) butter, cubed
a little rum or brandy
   (optional)

Heat the oven to 425°F, 220°C, gas mark 7. Take six pieces of silicone non-stick paper, and mark out an 8 inch (20 cm) circle on each. Ideally put each piece of paper on a metal baking sheet. If you only have two baking sheets just lay them out on the work surface.

Break the eggs into a mixing bowl, add the caster sugar, and whisk with an electric whisk on full speed until the mixture is light and foamy and the whisk just leaves a trail when lifted out of the mixture. Lightly fold in the sifted flour, a little at a time, with a metal spoon.

Divide the mixture between the six marked circles, spreading out evenly to fit the circles. Bake two at a time for about 6–10 minutes until pale golden and firm to the touch.

With a sharp knife, trim the circles to an even round. Peel off the paper and cool on a wire rack. Take one disc of sponge and put it on a piece of silicone paper, ready to top with the caramel. Lay out another sheet of silicone paper ready for the leftover caramel.

For the caramel, dissolve the sugar in the water over a low heat, then increase heat and boil until a deep straw colour. Allow to cool slightly then pour just over half of the caramel over the disc of sponge, then pour the remainder on to the second sheet of silicone paper. When the latter is set, just crush it up ready to decorate the sides of the cake. When the caramel on top of the sponge is just set, cut into eight, either with an oiled knife or oiled scissors.

For the butter cream, measure the cocoa into the processor, add the boiling water and mix for a moment then add the icing sugar and butter and process until smooth, adding a little rum or brandy if liked.

Sandwich the five rounds together with some of the butter cream and stand on a serving plate. Spread the top with some more butter cream and top with the eight caramel divisions. Spread the remaining butter cream around the sides, and press round the crushed caramel.

Serves 8

MILLEFEUILLES

I make this using bought puff pastry and home-made crème
pâtissière. *They are very messy to eat, so be sure to supply forks.
For extra effect, you could 'feather' the icing on the millefeuilles
instead of leaving it plain. Colour a tiny amount of the glacé
icing a different colour, and pipe in thin lines across the top of
the white icing; draw a pin through these lines at regular
intervals in the opposite direction to make a pretty pattern.*

1 × 8 oz (225 g) packet frozen
  puff pastry, thawed

Crème Pâtissière
2 eggs
2 oz (50 g) vanilla sugar (see
  page 9)
1 oz (25 g) flour
½ pint (300 ml) milk

Filling and Topping
raspberry jam
4 oz (100 g) icing sugar, sieved
lemon juice

Heat the oven to 450°F, 230°C, gas mark 8.

Roll the pastry out thickly on a lightly floured surface to a
rectangle 11 × 9 inches (28 × 23 cm). Lift on to a baking tray,
prick well with a fork and bake in the oven for about 12–15
minutes until well risen and golden brown. Cool on a wire rack
then cut in half lengthwise.

For the *crème pâtissière*, beat the eggs and sugar together with
the flour and a little of the milk. Heat the remaining milk in a
pan until almost boiling then pour on to the egg mixture,
stirring all the time. Return to the pan and heat gently, stirring
all the time until thickened. Remove from the heat and allow to
cool, stirring from time to time.

To assemble the millefeuilles, spread the top of one piece of
pastry with the jam and then with the *crème pâtissière*. Top
with the other piece of pastry and press lightly together.

Measure the icing sugar into a bowl and add just enough lemon juice to give a thick glacé icing. Coat the top of the millefeuilles and leave to set. Serve in slices.

Serves 6

GRIESTORTE

A Continental sponge with an almond flavour, it should be served straight from the refrigerator. Lemon cheese, bought from good supermarkets, contains the same ingredients as home-made lemon curd, and you can of course use this!

3 eggs, separated
4 oz (100 g) caster sugar
½ teaspoon almond essence
3 oz (75 g) semolina

Filling
¼ pint (150 ml) whipping
  cream
4 tablespoons lemon cheese
icing sugar

Heat the oven to 350°F, 180°C, gas mark 4. Grease and line an 8 inch (20 cm) round cake tin with greased greaseproof paper.

Measure the egg yolks and sugar into a bowl and whisk on full speed with an electric whisk until pale and thick. Fold in the almond essence and semolina. Whisk the egg whites in a separate bowl until they form soft peaks then gently fold into the mixture until blended.

Turn the mixture into the tin and bake in the oven for about 30 minutes or until well risen and pale golden brown. Turn out of the tin, peel off the paper and finish cooling on a wire rack.

Divide the cake in half horizontally. Whisk the cream until it forms soft peaks, then fold in the lemon cheese. Sandwich the cake back together with this mixture and keep in the refrigerator until required. Serve dusted with lots of icing sugar.

Serves 6

RUM BABAS

These rich yeast dough confections take time but are delicious as a special treat. If you like, leave out the currants, adding finely grated lemon rind instead.

4 oz (100 g) strong plain flour
½ oz (15 g) fresh yeast
3 tablespoons hand-hot milk
½ level teaspoon salt
1 tablespoon caster sugar
2 eggs
2 oz (50 g) butter, softened
2 oz (50 g) currants

Syrup
2 tablespoons each clear
    honey and water
1 tablespoon rum

To Decorate
¼ pint (150 ml) whipping
    cream, whipped

Lightly grease eight small ring moulds, and heat the oven to 400°F, 200°C, gas mark 6.

Measure 1 oz (25 g) of the flour, the yeast and hand-hot milk into a jug, whisk well until smooth then leave to stand in a warm place until frothy (about 10 minutes).

Put the remaining flour, salt, sugar, eggs, butter and currants into a bowl, add the frothy yeast liquid, and beat well for about 3 minutes with a wooden spoon. Half fill the ring moulds with the mixture, and stand on a baking tray. Cover lightly with a piece of oiled polythene and stand in a warm place until the mixture has risen to two-thirds up the sides of the moulds (about 40 minutes). Bake in the oven for 15–20 minutes until golden brown. Remove from the oven and leave to cool for a few moments then turn out of the moulds.

For the syrup, heat the honey and water together in a small pan, remove from the heat and stir in the rum. Whilst the babas are still warm, spoon over the syrup, then allow to cool completely. Arrange the babas on a serving plate and serve decorated with a little whipped cream.

Makes 8

SWISS CARROT CAKE

This really is gooey and delicious, and is my version of the carrot cake served après-ski *in Switzerland. Have it, as the Swiss do, with a cup of hot chocolate, topped with whipped cream and a sprinkling of chocolate powder. The yoghurt added to the topping gives a wonderful flavour.*

8 oz (225 g) self-raising flour
2 level teaspoons baking powder
5 oz (150 g) light muscovado sugar
2 oz (50 g) walnuts, chopped
4 oz (100 g) carrots, washed, trimmed and grated
2 ripe bananas, mashed

2 eggs
¼ pint (150 ml) sunflower oil

Topping
3 oz (75 g) soft margarine
3 oz (75 g) cream cheese
6 oz (175 g) icing sugar, sieved
4 tablespoons plain yoghurt

Heat the oven to 350°F, 180°C, gas mark 4, and grease and line an 8 inch (20 cm) round cake tin with greased greaseproof paper.

Measure the flour and baking powder into a large bowl and stir in the sugar. Add the nuts, carrot and banana, and mix lightly. Make a well in the centre, add the eggs and oil, and beat well until blended.

Turn into the tin and bake in the oven for about 1¼ hours until the cake is golden brown, and is shrinking slightly from the sides of the tin. A warm skewer pushed into the centre should come out clean. Turn out, remove the paper, and leave to cool on a wire rack.

For the topping, measure all the ingredients together in a bowl and beat well until blended and smooth. Spread over the cake and rough up with a fork. Leave in a cool place to harden slightly before serving. Serve cut into thin wedges.

CONTINENTAL CHEESECAKE

A smashing cooked cheesecake. If liked, add 6 oz (175 g)
sultanas to the cheesecake mixture with the egg whites before
baking.

Crust
3 oz (75 g) digestive biscuits,
  crushed
1½ (40 g) butter, melted
1 oz (25 g) demerara sugar

Cheesecake
2 oz (50 g) soft margarine
6 oz (175 g) caster sugar
1 lb (450 g) curd cheese
1 oz (25 g) flour
finely grated rind and juice of
  1 lemon

3 eggs, separated
5 fl oz (150 ml) double cream,
  lightly whipped

Topping
1 × 15 oz (425 g) can
  blackcurrants or stoned
  black cherries
1 heaped teaspoon arrowroot
a little Kirsch

Heat the oven to 325°F, 160°C, gas mark 3. Lightly oil a 9 inch
(23 cm) loose-bottomed cake tin, and line with greased greaseproof paper. (You do need to line a loose-bottomed tin properly
as the mixture is slack when it goes into the tin and it may seep
through the bottom (see page 13).

Mix together the ingredients for the crust, spread over the base
of the tin and press down firmly with the back of a metal spoon.
Leave to set.

Measure the margarine, sugar, curd cheese, flour, rind, juice
and egg yolks into a large bowl. Beat until smooth. Fold in the
cream. Whisk the egg whites stiffly then fold into the mixture.
Pour on to the crust.

Bake in the oven for about an hour until set. Turn off the oven
and leave in the oven for a further hour to cool. Run a knife

round the edge of the tin, push the base up through the cake tin, and remove the side paper.

To decorate, thicken the juice of the fruit with the arrowroot, slurping in a dash of Kirsch for added flavour! Pile on top of the cheesecake.

Serves 10

VACHERIN

This is a meringue topped with a thick chestnut cream. Make the meringues well beforehand, then assemble the vacherin half an hour before you serve it. If you want to make this look very special, put the chestnut filling in a piping bag with a small plain nozzle, and pipe in squiggles into a mountain shape.

Meringue
3 egg whites
6 oz (175 g) caster sugar

Chestnut Filling
1 × 8 oz (225 g) can
   sweetened chestnut purée
½ pint (300 ml) whipping
   cream, whipped
2 tablespoons sherry

Heat the oven to 225°F, 110°C, gas mark ¼, and line a baking sheet with silicone paper. Draw an 8 inch (20 cm) circle on the paper.

Whisk the egg whites with an electric whisk until they form soft peaks, then whisk in the sugar a teaspoonful at a time. Whisk well after each addition until all the sugar has been added.

Use half the meringue to fill the circle on the paper, and level out evenly. Put spoonfuls of the remaining meringue on to the rest of the paper in six heaps, drawing them up to a peak with the handle of a teaspoon.

Bake the meringues in the oven for about 3 hours until they are crisp, firm and an off-white colour. Remove from the oven and leave to cool, then carefully peel off the paper.

To serve, put the chestnut purée into a bowl and fold in the whipped cream and sherry. Put the meringue base on to a serving plate, pile the filling on to the meringue and arrange the small meringues around the edge.

Serves 6

VIENNESE TEA CAKES

Always popular for tea time or coffee mornings. They can be piped in finger-shaped biscuits on to a greased baking tray and dipped in melted plain chocolate if you want a change.

6 oz (175 g) butter
2 oz (50 g) icing sugar
¼ teaspoon vanilla essence

6 oz (175 g) plain flour
sieved icing sugar and red jam
   for decoration

Stand about 10 paper baking cases in a 12-hole bun tin, and heat the oven to 350°F, 180°C, gas mark 4.

Measure the butter and icing sugar into a bowl and beat until light and creamy. Add the vanilla essence and gradually work in the flour.

Using a piping bag and large star nozzle, pipe the mixture into the cases in a circular shape leaving a slight dip in the centre. Bake in the oven for about 20 minutes until just beginning to colour.

Lift the cakes on to a cooling tray and when cool dust lightly with icing sugar. Finish with a dot of red jam in the hollow in the centre.

Makes about 10

FRENCH TARTLETS

Make these as little round tartlets or as boat shapes, depending on what moulds you have available.

Pastry Cases
8 oz (225 g) plain flour
6 oz (175 g) butter
1 oz (25 g) caster sugar
1 egg yolk
about 2 tablespoons water

Apricot Filling
2 oz (50 g) almond paste (see page 122)
4 fresh apricots, skinned and sliced
2 tablespoons apricot jam

Strawberry Filling
2 tablespoons redcurrant jelly
8 oz (225 g) small whole fresh strawberries

Heat the oven to 425°F, 220°C, gas mark 7.

Measure the flour into a bowl and rub in the butter until the mixture resembles fine breadcrumbs. Stir in the sugar then bind together with the egg yolk and water to give a firm dough. Wrap in clear film and chill for about 30 minutes.

Turn out on to a lightly floured surface, and knead lightly. Roll out and use to line as many tartlet or boat moulds as you have. Line each with a small piece of foil, and stand on a baking tray. Bake for about 12 minutes, removing the foil for the last 5 minutes, until the pastry is golden brown. Allow to cool, then lift out of the moulds on to a cooling rack.

Gently heat the redcurrant jelly, and brush a little on the inside of half the moulds, arrange the strawberries inside, and spoon over the remaining glaze. For the remaining moulds, put a sliver of almond paste in the bottom of each, top with a few slices of apricot, then glaze with a little warmed apricot jam.

Arrange on a serving plate and serve with a little cream.

Makes about 20 tartlets

DANISH PASTRIES

Now easier and quicker to make since the new fast dried yeast arrived. You simply mix it with the flour – no mixing with water and sugar and then waiting for action! Always serve the pastries warm. (They freeze well!)

Pastry
8 oz (225 g) strong plain flour
¼ teaspoon salt
6 oz (175 g) butter
1 packet McDougalls fast
   action dried yeast
5 tablespoons hand-hot water
1 egg
1 oz (25 g) caster sugar
a little beaten egg, to glaze

Filling and Topping
4 oz (100 g) white almond
   paste (see page 122)
a little glacé icing made with
   4 oz (100 g) icing sugar
1 oz (25 g) toasted flaked
   almonds
1 oz (25 g) glacé cherries,
   washed, dried and chopped

Measure the flour and salt into a large bowl and rub in 1 oz (25 g) of the butter. Add the packet of yeast and blend in. Make a well in the centre, add the water and the egg blended with the sugar. Draw in the flour from the sides and mix to a soft dough. Turn out on to a floured surface and knead. Slip into a polythene bag and chill for 10 minutes.

Mash the remaining butter until it is spreadable. Take the chilled dough from the fridge and roll out to an oblong about 12 × 10 inches (30 × 25 cm). Spread the butter down the centre of the dough. Fold the two long sides of the pastry inwards so that they are just overlapping to encase the butter. Fold the length of dough into three as you would for flaky pastry. Return to the polythene bag and chill for a further 10 minutes. Roll out again to an oblong then fold into three. Repeat this process and chill again for 10 minutes.

Makes 16

To make Croissant Shapes

Take half the pastry and roll out to a 9 inch (23 cm) circle. Divide the circle into eight. Place a small amount of almond paste at the wide end of each wedge, and brush with beaten egg. Roll them up from this end towards the point, and bend them into a crescent shape.

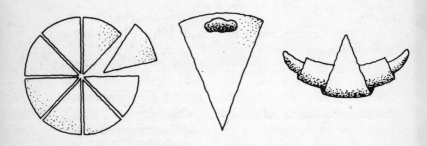

To make Star Shapes

Roll out half the remaining dough to form a 6 inch (15 cm) square. Cut the square into four. Place a small amount of almond paste in the centre of one square. Make cuts from each corner almost to the centre, brush with beaten egg, then lift the left-hand corner of the bottom triangle on to the centre to cover part of the almond paste. Repeat with the other three triangles to form a star. Shape the remaining squares in the same way.

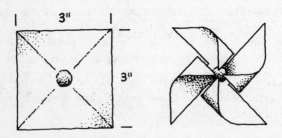

To make Kite Shapes

Roll out the remaining dough very thinly to form an 8 inch (20 cm) square. Cut the square into four. Place a small amount of almond paste on the centre of one square. Cut ½ inch (1.5 cm) inside the square as shown, A to B and C to D, then brush with beaten egg. Lift both cut corner strips at E and cross them over the almond paste in the centre. Repeat this with the remaining squares.

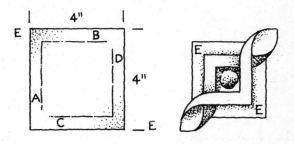

To bake

Heat the oven to 425°F, 220°C, gas mark 7.

Arrange the pastries on baking trays, cover with polythene, and leave to prove for about 20 minutes in a warm place until beginning to look puffy.

Brush each with beaten egg again, and bake in the oven for about 15 minutes until golden brown. Lift on to a wire rack to cool.

Spoon a little of the icing over each pastry whilst they are still warm. Sprinkle some of them with flaked almonds and some with small pieces of glacé cherries.

INDEX